W9-CKL-321

Other physical fitness books by
Curtis Mitchell

JOY OF JOGGING
PUT YOURSELF IN SHAPE
FITNESS FOR THE WHOLE FAMILY (with Paul Dudley White)

# THE PERFECT EXERCISE

**The Hop, Skip, and Jump Way to Health**

CURTIS MITCHELL

A.C.S.M.

Illustrations by
JUDY FRANCIS

**Simon and Schuster • New York**

Published by Simon and Schuster
A Gulf+Western Company
Rockefeller Center, 630 Fifth Avenue
New York, New York 10020

Designed by Eve Metz
Manufactured in the United States of America

1 2 3 4 5 6 7 8 9 10

Library of Congress Cataloging in Publication Data

Mitchell, Curtis.
The perfect exercise.

Bibliography: p. 185
1. Exercise. 2. Rope skipping. 3. Hygiene.
I. Title.
RA781.M57 613.7'1 75-38844
ISBN 0-671-22176-0


Table on p. 154 prepared by Robert E. Johnson, M.D., Ph.D., and colleagues, Department of Physiology and Biophysics, University of Illinois, August, 1967.

Dedicated to the memory of
PAUL DUDLEY WHITE, M.D.
inspiring friend,
collaborator, and perennial apostle
of fitness through physical activity

# CONTENTS

# ACKNOWLEDGMENTS

Every day during a book's gestation, a writer incurs debts. A letter from a friend, a smile from a waitress, a compliment from a clerk, a jubilant remark from a member of the family—these all keep him going, and they can never be repaid.

The roots of my gratitude reach back to so many, I regret that I can name only a few. Among them are:

Kaare Rodahl, M.D., of the Institute for Work Physiology, Oslo, Norway, who encouraged me to begin jumping rope.

John H. Allen, Assistant Managing Editor of the *Reader's Digest*, who urged me to write about it.

Charles R. Williams, Vice-President and Director of Sales, Simon and Schuster, Inc., who suggested that skipping rope was a subject big enough for a book.

H. Harrison Clarke, Ph.D., of the University of Oregon, Eugene; Bruno Balke, M.D., of the University of Wisconsin, Madison; Lawrence Golding, Ph.D., of Kent State University, Kent, Ohio; Thomas K. Cureton, Ph.D., of the University of Illinois, Urbana—all great physiologists who have shared their knowledge and wisdom over many years.

Kenneth Cooper, M.D., founder of the Aerobics Center and the Institute for Aerobic Research, Dallas, Texas, whose writing and example have inspired so many.

Frank Prentup, of the University of Colorado, Boulder, and Paul Smith, of the Shoreline Public Schools, Seattle, Washington, who have taught more people to skip than anyone else I know.

Fran Carlton, of TV's "Fran Carlton Show," Orlando, Florida;

**ACKNOWLEDGMENTS**

Jack Baker, Ph.D., Murray State University, Murray, Kentucky; and Vojin Smodlaka, M.D., Methodist Hospital, Brooklyn, N.Y., who guided me through sundry perplexities.

Sara Staff Jernigan, professor of physical education, and Eleanor Anne Hurst, circulation librarian, of Stetson University, DeLand, Florida, who provided access to both scientific and recreational aspects of skipping.

Nan A. Talese, my editor with Simon and Schuster, Inc., who was always encouraging and supportive.

And last but not least, Zelpha, my beloved wife, secretary, and critic who while discharging her duties never once forgot to smile.

C.M.

# Preface

For many years I have advocated exercise and fitness. During that time, hundreds of people have asked, "What is the one *best* exercise?" At last I have an answer.

It is *jumping rope*.

My reasons for this choice are that, invariably, the results of jumping are good, the effort and time required are minimal, and I am never bored. Much scientific investigation and expert opinion support my conclusion.

If you wonder how a layman and a writer can make such a claim, let me qualify myself. Since becoming an investigative reporter two decades ago, I have searched steadily for mental and physical programs that might improve the quality of my life. During that period, I have seen increasing stresses and tensions take a larger and larger toll of unfit men and women. The big killer among my personal friends, as in all America, has been the heart attack. In the early sixties, I heard about a group of middle-aged men working in Cleveland who had become so fit through vigorous exercise that even the professional athletes of the famous Cleveland Browns football team could not match their pace. I went out to investigate.

All of those "elderly" exercisers were desk and office workers. Several had suffered heart attacks. Other past illnesses ranged from ulcers to arthritis. I found the men red-cheeked, vigorous, and enthusiastic. Their daily workouts included calisthenics, jogging, and swimming, which they performed in a novel manner, working in short bursts of furious activity followed by catch-up periods of slow movement. Work and rest, work and rest, over and over. It was a new kind of workout, and it was the secret both of their physical improvement and of their immunity from organic damage. At the time, I did not understand it, nor did most physicians and physiologists. We are wiser now.

Significantly, repeated short energy bursts are what happens when you exercise with a jump rope. After my discovery in Cleveland I became a student of health and exercise, reading medical and physiological textbooks and interviewing American and international authorities. I met Dr. Paul Dudley White, America's foremost heart specialist and a persistent exponent of exercise, and we collaborated on several magazine articles and eventually a book.

But many of the people I met still had one argument against exercise that I could not answer. "I agree with what you say," they explained, "but I can't find the time."

I had no answer because everyone knew that exercise works slowly, secretly. Dr. White had said, "The type of exercise doesn't matter. What matters is that it should be vigorous from childhood on, and performed for at least an hour a day."

Dr. Kenneth Cooper, whose book *Aerobics* sent a million desk jockeys onto the jogging paths, prescribed a point system that ate up time and put the average man's fitness a long way down the road.

Dr. Thomas Cureton, of the University of Illinois, a physical fitness pioneer, demanded sixty-minute sessions; in a pinch, no less than thirty.

Prof. Per-Olof Astrand, M.D., Sweden's great authority,

considered thirty minutes three times a week minimal.

So thousands of persons who wanted to exercise still could find no program that would fit into their busy lives. A year or so ago, I joined them. After years of jogging, I became an exercise drop-out. Though I told myself, "I'll start again next week," I was always too tired or too busy.

Alternatives were no better. Tennis was a problem because of the difficulty of finding partners. Hiking consumed too much time. Bicycling took me down streets where large dogs attacked my legs and feet, finally sending me to a hospital for emergency repairs. A daily trek to a gym or spa was out of the question. With my mental and physical reserves declining, I knew I quickly had to find a suitable program.

During the years of my involvement with physiological change through exercise, several clues had lodged in my unconscious. Now they emerged.

A weary grandmother who had planned to retire from her teaching job had begun to skip rope a few minutes each day. Her newfound zest launched her into a revitalized career.

A physician, Dr. Kaare Rodahl, then at Philadelphia's famous Lankenau Hospital, had told me of experimenting with a group of tired hospital workers, who were persuaded to jump rope for a few minutes each day. Their fitness and endurance improved by an average of 25 percent. Later, Dr. Rodahl wrote a fine book about exercise which made rope jumping the core of a program for healthful living.

Canadian scientists had found that an exercise program with sessions as brief as two-and-one-half to five minutes would produce important improvements in strength and endurance.

A German scientist claimed that a single burst of exercise lasting only three minutes would help protect the heart.

A young university researcher had published the generally disregarded news that his laboratory tests of rope jumping proved it to be up to four times as effective as jogging.

But skipping rope? Wasn't that for kids? I recalled that

boxing champions, without exception, had included rope skipping in their training programs. But would it work for an average, middle-aged John Doe (or a young married person, or a senior citizen) who had little time? Would it hold my interest?

Wondering, I bought a length of sash cord, made myself a jump rope, and embarked on a bobtailed program. And I was hooked.

Jumping a rope, which is so simple and easy, produces an astonishing reaction in the body and mind. One result seems to be that nerves, muscles, and circulation are so stimulated by short bursts of honest-to-goodness exercise (one cannot rest while jumping) that they improve at a gratifying rate.

Joggers who jump rope improve in strength and endurance.

Golfers develop stronger wrists and better eye–hand coordination.

Tennis players strengthen their grip and learn to change directions more rapidly.

Older persons acquire flexibility in their joints.

Everyone suffers less from fatigue.

A cardiac's damaged heart muscle is restored to normal strength.

Boredom is banished by the challenge of acquiring new steps, jumps, and whirls.

Privacy is possible because you can jump rope in your garage or kitchen.

When I first began to skip, I expected physical changes. But what surprised me was the mental stimulus, the "lift" that came with each session. The rope whirls, leg muscles tense and relax, the feet skip over the rope with almost no room to spare, and somehow I know that I am in tune with elemental rhythms. And I feel secure.

Part One

# BACKGROUND FOR A PERFECT EXERCISE

# 1

# Hop, Skip, and Jump to Health

We don't wear out, we rust out, according to Dr. Theodore G. Klump. "I am convinced that one who sits and waits for death to come along will not have long to wait."

This rusting process—called *atherosclerosis*—already afflicts the arteries of most adult Americans and kills approximately one million of us each year. Even young people are endangered. "It will come as a shock to the sedentary American male that his body is middle-aged by the time he is twenty-six," according to Dr. Thomas Kirk Cureton, retired chief of the Physical Fitness Research Center at the University of Illinois. Middle age at twenty-six? He was referring to the careful research of Dr. Hardin Jones, University of California, who had found that the flow of blood through the muscles of an eighteen-year-old boy averaged 25 cubic centimeters per minute. By age twenty-five, the flow had decreased to 16cc., a 40 percent drop. By age thirty-five, it was down to 10cc. More recent research seems to indicate an even earlier drop. Today babies are being born with atherosclerosis.

"I have two doctors, my right leg and my left," said Dr. George Macaulay Trevelyan. "When body and mind are out of gear, I know that I have only to call in my doctors and I shall be well again."

Dr. Paul Dudley White spoke of the legs as a "second heart." The leg muscles are the body's largest. Literally thousands of miles of blood vessels penetrate them, dividing and subdividing into branches and tributaries and tiny rivulets until each bundle of muscle cells and each nerve cell is bathed in a food-rich river. Teach the muscles of the legs to work more efficiently, drawing food more quickly from the tide of blood and discharging more waste products into the passing flood, and a feeling of well-being spreads over the whole body. All authorities agree on the importance of leg work. No system of exercise omits it. As every sports fan knows, it is true that "when the legs go, the body goes." Bruce Barton, advertising genius of an earlier decade, applied that principle to business. "If you want to know about a man's mind," he said, "feel his legs."

In recent years, the unprecedented interest in exercise programs has become a testimony to our sedentary entanglements. Exercise physiologists have prescribed such newfangled procedures as isometrics and aerobics and such old-fangled ones as yoga and calisthenics. Our parks are full of joggers, bicyclists, and little old ladies in tennis shoes.

Skipping rope provides the most concentrated leg exercise of all, plus there is a bonus which results from moving your hands, wrists, and arms against the centrifugal force generated by a revolving 9-foot jump rope. Improbable as it seems, the reaction spreads from the fingers up the arms to the shoulders, across the back and down the rib cage. This means that both the lower and the upper body benefit. One weight lifter even trains with a jump rope because of its head-to-toe upbuilding. But he uses, instead of a sash cord, a 45-pound chain.

What benefits does an ordinary jump rope bring?

First, it reduces fat on legs, thighs, hips. Second, it increases agility and improves the sense of balance. It also adds strength to muscles all over the body.

You need no special equipment except a length of sash cord, and no special clothing. You can jump almost anywhere, so it is also convenient. In Orlando, Florida, Fran Carlton, who is famous as the star of "The Fran Carlton Exercise Show" on southern radio and TV stations, adopted rope jumping when she learned through experience that jogging with her husband was not her thing. "I decided there had to be a better way," she says, recalling unfriendly dogs and wet trails, "so I bought a jump rope." Now while her husband is doing his two-mile jog in the morning, Fran Carlton jumps in her air-conditioned kitchen. In five minutes she gets all the exercise she needs to tone her muscles and protect her heart. By the time her husband returns, she has showered, dressed, and is ready for business.

Those who think rope skipping is for children should visit some of our universities. John Wooten, former Cleveland Browns guard, first learned about skipping rope while attending Colorado University. Big and burly, he was so awkward during his first season, his coach reports, that he could hardly lead interference. Rope skipping was prescribed, and it turned his career around. "How that boy could run," his coach recalls. "He got so handy with his feet he could run over a crate of eggs without cracking a shell."

Once one becomes adept, the game turns into a sport and then into a challenge. *The Guinness Book of World Records* says that J. P. Hughes, of Melbourne, Australia, skipped for 32,089 turns without missing. It took three hours and ten minutes. Another Australian zoomed to a speed record by making 286 turns in one minute. In Japan, one Suzuki leaped so high that he made 5 turns in a single jump. *Sports Illustrated* reported recently that this same Suzuki skipped 37,427 times in four hours, twenty-two minutes and fifty seconds, shattering the former world record held by an American rabbi. Finally, an Australian named Tommy Morris skipped rope for 1,000 miles, hopping from Melbourne to Adelaide and back.

At the University of Colorado, retired baseball coach Frank Prentup has a group of girls who can probably outskip any prizefighter that ever lived. The usual fighter can do about four skipping variations. Prentup's pupils can do fifty-two. Exercise physiologist Jack Baker, head of the Human Performance Laboratory of Murray State University in Kentucky, has done experiments showing that about the same level of fitness is achieved with ten minutes of skipping as with thirty minutes of jogging.

Dr. Kaare Rodahl, who is currently the director of the Institute of Work Physiology in Oslo, Norway, says that 500 hops in five minutes (three or four times per week) will maintain a satisfactory level.

Hopping seems to be nature's outlet for the tension felt by all human beings. Evidence can be seen any weekend afternoon during the football season. Cheerleaders bounce like Yo-Yos. In a tight game, following a crucial touchdown, winning players leap about. The same thing happens in soccer, baseball, and wherever else it becomes necessary to blow off steam. Even on a TV money show, when a contestant hits a jackpot, he leaps up. We also use phrases to express the feeling of tension release, to wit: "Jumping Jehosephat!" and "Jumping Jiminy."

Nobody knows where rope skipping started, but explorers have returned from expeditions to tell of aborigines joyously jumping over jungle vines and flexible strips of bamboo. Pictures of medieval life shows tiny tots rolling hoops and jumping ropes.

In the 1960s it was Dr. Rodahl who organized what was probably the first group of typical working women to be scientifically tested in the United States. Their ages ranged from nineteen to forty-two years. Their previous activity had included hospital duties, housework, and walking to the bus. They would skip rope for five minutes daily, five times each week, for four weeks.

Skeptics were convinced that nothing would happen. When careful measurements of key fitness indices were compared (before and after), the once-fatigued ladies had achieved a breakthrough. Those least fit had improved the most, and those most fit had improved the least, but *all had improved.*

Dr. Rodahl described his findings. "During the first week of training," he said, "the mean pulse . . . at the fifth minute of rope skipping was one hundred sixty-eight beats per minute. During the last week of training, it was one hundred forty-five beats per minute." (A lowered pulse rate is a sure sign of improved endurance and organic reserve.)

To cross-check his figures, the doctor had also tested a control group of women of similar ages and backgrounds, but who didn't skip rope. Their retest at the end of the fourth week showed no pulse rate improvement whatever.

Statistically speaking, his rope-skipping workers had increased their average fitness by a huge 25 percent. This was astounding, considering the brevity of the exercise period. Needless to say, all their midafternoon blahs had long since disappeared, their work had improved, and so had their mental approach to their problems.

Earlier, a little-known but significant experiment had been completed at the University of Illinois by graduate student John T. Powell. Working out of the Illinois Physical Fitness Research Center, Powell invited five youths about ten years of age to participate in a unique project. First each boy's level of fitness was ascertained, and then he was given a jump rope. He was asked to practice three activities every day.

1. To perform as many skips as possible without missing.
2. To do as many turns as possible in five successive efforts.
3. To do as many skips as possible in sixty minutes.

The boys jumped five days each week for ten weeks. The results were astonishing. Overall, they had grown like saplings in the spring. Their physical changes included greater leg and knee strength, increased calf size, better jumping ability (some could jump 4½ inches higher), and faster running speed. They were more agile, more flexible, and their shoulders had broadened (which surprised the experts), and their chests had deepened. Their hearts, instead of being strained as some old-school doctors had feared, had become vastly stronger.

Some time later, Arthur Cascino supervised a similar training program using adults at Temple University in Philadelphia. His subjects were between nineteen and forty-three years old. They all improved dramatically in a pattern that followed that of the Illinois boys. Again, the overall improvement in endurance averaged about 25 percent.

Beyond doubt, skipping rope really worked. All ages and both sexes could do it. It saved time and money and could be done anywhere. From his view of the field of muscle physiology, Dr. Rodahl said, "There is no more efficient way you can possibly use the time." Skipping rope was, in fact, the perfect exercise—waiting to be discovered.

## EXERCISES COMPARED

Dr. Kenneth Cooper, author of *Aerobics* and founder of the Institute for Aerobics Research in Dallas, Texas, has invented (and made famous) a point system which measures the effectiveness of various kinds of exercise.

Hereunder are several popular exercises as rated by his point system and published in *Aerobics, The New Aerobics,* and other scientific literature.

**HOP, SKIP, AND JUMP TO HEALTH**

| Activity | Time | Point Value |
|---|---|---|
| Jumping rope | 10 minutes | 3 points* |
| Jogging, 1 mile | 10 minutes | 3 points |
| Tennis, singles | 1 20-minute set | 1½ points |
| Swimming, 300 yards | 10 minutes | 1 point |
| Bicycling, 2 miles | 8 to 10 minutes | 1 point |
| Handball | 10 minutes | 1½ points |
| Walking, stroll | 1 hour | 1½ points |
| Golf, 18 holes (no cart) | 4 hours | 3 points |
| Skiing, water or snow | 30 minutes | 3 points |
| Square dancing | 30 minutes | 2½ points |

* Other scientific evidence has reported that jumping rope for 10 minutes is as effective in conditioning the body as approximately 30 minutes of jogging. See page 154.

# 2

# What Exercise Does

The difference between exercise and other cures for illness and fatigue is that exercise treats the whole person, not just a part, using the body's built-in therapy and man's oldest remedy, which is a solution, slightly salty, called blood. Exercise creates better blood and moves it to wherever it is needed.

A decade ago, an unusual thing happened: A concerned government officially endorsed the idea of strenuous activity and provided a practical program for its citizens. That was when Canada's Royal Air Force offered to everyone the regime with which it had trained its pilots. It was the famous 5BX plan. Canadian physiologists even claimed that it was never too late to begin exercising. Regardless of age, exercise would do such things as:

. . . increase the strength of important muscles
. . . increase the speed of their response
. . . keep joints flexible
. . . improve the efficiency of the heart, lungs, and other organs
. . . increase one's capacity for sports
. . . relieve back pain by strengthening back muscles

... make one less likely to be injured
... assure more rapid recovery, if injured
... help to control unwanted fat deposits
... reduce nervous tension and emotional upsets.

Soon the U.S. Government climbed on the bandwagon. Under President Kennedy, it published its own fitness manual, called *Adult Physical Fitness,* which went further than the Canadians. It promised:

... improved posture
... fewer aches and pains, less stiffness and soreness
... increased efficiency in performing physical work
... less chronic fatigue.

"The evidence is conclusive," said Uncle Sam, "that individuals who consistently engage in proper physical activity have better job performance records, fewer degenerative diseases, and probably a longer life expectancy than the population at large. By delaying the aging process, proper exercise also prolongs your active years."

And one of the exercises recommended officially for both men and women was skipping rope.

Experts agree that fitness is largely the result of two factors:

1. Good circulation
2. A strong heart

You are able to move your body only because the food you have eaten combines with the oxygen carried by your bloodstream to produce heat and energy. If it happened in a haystack, you would call it spontaneous combustion.

Saying it another way, your energy comes from billions of tiny fires which ignite spontaneously when the oxygen in your blood combines with the nutrients stored in your cells. Oxygen is the catalyst. Because oxygen is present in the air, you can light a candle in the darkness. Because oxygen is present in your blood, you can light a fire in your heart.

Your problem (everybody's problem) is moving that oxygen to where it is needed. Your circulation does this, picking up oxygen from the air you breathe as your blood streams through your lungs. Passing into your cells (which are miniature combustion chambers), the combination of food (fuel) and oxygen ignites and turns to heat and energy.

That is half the story.

## HOW STRONG IS YOUR HEART?

The heart is a double-barreled pump the size of your fist. Each time it beats, its left side drives a large jigger of blood into the hoselike blood vessel that climbs toward the throat and then turns downward, branching into conduits to the brain and the body, thence to seek out every nook and cranny of your tissue. Each time it beats, its right side pumps a jigger of tired and syrupy blood through your lungs for cleansing. Seventy-two times a minute, a hundred thousand times a day, two and a half billion times in one life's span. The work involved is unbelievable.

Is your heart strong enough to pump enough blood to carry enough oxygen to burn enough food to create enough energy to accomplish the work you want to do?

The energetic have efficient oxygen-transport systems driven by powerful, durable hearts. The unfit have inefficient systems and "office" hearts. The fit have energy enough and to spare. The unfit run a deficit by midday and are exhausted by evening.

That's it. The heart pumps and the blood flows. Oxygen from the blood lights tiny fires in a billion cells. Stepping up this process is what turns fatness into fitness. Or fatigue into vigor. Or worry into joy.

Exercise offers other gifts:

The volume of your blood increases.

Millions of new red corpuscles emerge from bone marrow and join the bloodstream, reviving tired blood.

Fatty substances in your blood (cholesterol and triglycerides) are reduced, thus lessening the danger of arterial blockage.

New capillaries open in your muscles, adding their miniature conduits to your humming vascular network.

Your cells convert food and oxygen into energy more rapidly.

These events occur almost without your knowing. What you do know is that you feel better. You may have fewer headaches, less back pain, and lower blood pressure. Many studies provide scientific proof of these changes. A fit person is less likely to suffer a fatal heart attack. If you do have an attack, your chance of survival is better and your recovery is faster. You convert fat into solid muscle and you play games better.

Will you live longer if you exercise? Many factors are involved, including your family tree. Long-lived ancestors are especially helpful. Perhaps the best answer now available is the one YMCA experts have used for decades. They say, "Exercise may not add years to your life, but it sure adds life to your years."

All these facts about fitness have been known by the experts and disregarded by the public for a long time. Young men are the worst offenders. They dot the landscape every weekend. Some are hitting small white balls, others are batting larger white balls. Their hectic activities inspired Dr. Warren Guild, of Boston, to utter the classic comment, "Don't ever worry about when a weekend athlete will have a heart attack. He'll have it on a weekend."

People flock to our beaches, but the surf is never crowded. Groups cluster around swimming pools from coast to coast but rarely go near the water.

The body must move vigorously to be worthy of survival.

Inaction always demands a penalty. Professor Arthur H. Steinhaus, when at George Williams College, gave a demonstration to prove the point. Choosing the huskiest student in the class, he would lash him tightly to an upright board so he could not move a muscle. Within minutes, the student always fainted. His blood had pooled in his legs, starving the heart and the head. So the brain "blacked out." Every day, if you don't move enough, you starve your brain. Each passing day and year the sludge builds up. The penalty? Dizzy spells, at least; at worst, a stroke or death.

Decay is so easy to encourage. Inactivity is the trigger. Without work to do, the heart becomes smaller and less efficient. Unused bones release calcium and become brittle. Your less efficient heart pumps less blood. As the bloodstream slows, it delivers less oxygen and eliminates less waste. Internal organs suffer from the spreading blight; filter systems become clogged; capillary canals close up, cheating tissues of needed nourishment.

All this can happen while you are making up your mind to begin an exercise program. Thirty days of bed rest, they say, will cost you four-fifths of your ability to perform your day-to-day duties.

The alternative is work. Lots of work! So said Dr. Tom Cureton, whose popular fitness program demanded an hour a day of calisthenics, stretching, deep breathing, walking, jogging, and sometimes swimming. When I visited one of his classes some years ago and asked his students what they got out of exercise, I got these blunt answers:

"My greatest change is a new feeling of well-being."

"I've got more energy and drive, and greater self-confidence."

"I'm more willing to accept demanding challenges."

"I'm more optimistic."

"I'm not so tense."

"I feel great all the time."

"I fall asleep sooner and don't require so much sleep."

"I never get tired any more, and I've stopped cursing red traffic lights."

And one man told us, "My wife tells me I've quit snoring."

Consistent, continuous, rhythmic work made those changes.

Several years ago, physiologists and physicians from all over the world attended a world congress for sports medicine in Hanover, Germany. They discussed the mysteries of exercising the human body. I was a listener. Leaving the United States, I had been a member of the grunt-and-groan school of exercisers.

I came back with IT.

IT stands for Interval Training, which is simply an incredibly efficient way of increasing the body's fitness.

In Europe IT was an old story. Physical directors and trainers knew all about it. When I asked them, "How much exercise must I do each day to become fit?" their answers startled me. Five minutes . . . three . . . even fifteen seconds, they said. I couldn't believe it.

Let me review IT's history. Paavo Nurmi, who won the Olympic mile for Finland in 1920 (and every other international event he entered), had trained himself by using alternate work and rest periods. His coach called it "terrace" training, because you exercise at one level and then, when your body has adjusted to the work, you climb up to a higher level or terrace. Nurmi's phenomenal success attracted so much attention that physiological laboratories throughout Europe began to experiment with his method. Sweden adopted Interval Training and produced the next super-runner. Germany followed with several champions. Then World War II wiped out European athletics and Interval Training.

One of the survivors was old Professor Gerschler, director of the Institute of Physical Education of Freiburg University, who turned IT into a science.

Together with a celebrated cardiologist, Dr. H. Reindell,

he tested 3,000 subjects and came up with a training program that consisted of a *fifteen-second* period of running followed by a ninety-second rest period, both repeated often enough to elevate the heart rate to a training level. Soon swimmers, milers, and marathoners in many countries were experimenting with their own modifications, and Interval Training was established as a miracle technique.

Why did it work so well? What was so special about this work-and-rest formula? Dr. Gerschler said it was because the heart grew stronger, not while laboring, but during the recovery period. Therefore, the exercise regimen should include many recovery periods.

But why did the heart grow stronger during the rest interval? It was a paradox. Soon meticulous research provided an answer. This laboratory experiment did it.

An Interval Training physiologist named Karrasch brought an athlete to his laboratory and put him astride an exercise bicycle. The scientist set a difficult work load of many foot-pounds. "Pedal five minutes and then rest," he ordered. The athlete obeyed. After two pedaling sessions (a total of ten minutes), he was exhausted. His pulse rate was 170 beats per minute.

After recovery, the athlete was directed to pedal the same work load for two minutes (instead of five), followed by a rest of three minutes, and to repeat the pattern as long as possible. This time he managed twelve exercise-and-rest bouts, and he had accomplished much more work. Again, his heart rate was 170 beats.

Finally the subject was told to pedal the same work load for thirty seconds and rest for forty-five seconds and to repeat the pattern as long as he felt like it. This time he continued the experiment through forty-eight bouts, surpassing all the work he had previously done *without any feeling of fatigue.* This time his pulse never rose above 100. When they called off the experiment, he was still raring to go.

I find it interesting that big business in the United States discovered this truth years ago. A steel company hired an efficiency expert to improve the productivity of its workers. They were managing to move an average of 12½ tons of steel per man per day. All the workers complained of fatigue from early morning until quitting time. Each load they lifted tried their strength to its limit. The expert planned a routine that cut down load weight so it could be easily handled. A single steelworker was assigned to the new schedule—with an amazing result. While the regular laborers were moving their 12½ tons, the converted worker moved an unbelievable 47 tons. Easily, without ever tiring.

So there is a better way to exercise. Its name is Interval Training. Its recipe for success: if the task looks too big, just "nibble" at it.

A German physiologist helped me to understand it. He suggested taking the process step by step.

1. Your objective is to strengthen the heart.
2. You strengthen the heart muscle when you feed it plenty of oxygen and when you work it.
3. Oxygen is extracted from the air you breathe as your blood moves through the lungs. Your red blood cells pick it up and distribute it throughout the heart muscle and wherever else it is needed.
4. This distribution is made possible by the beating of your blood-pump, the heart.
5. So the heart is the key to fitness. The stronger the heart, the more work you can perform.

Okay, you say! But how does the above circular process *strengthen* the heart?

What follows may be more than you want to know.

## THE EXERCISE BOUT

Your heart-pump speeds up, driving blood into the arteries. Your muscles receive it and then your muscle-pumps drive it through your veins toward the heart. Your diaphragm (the largest muscle-pump) thrusts it back into your heart. Think of your circulating blood as a sort of liquid flywheel whirling through your body.

## THE RECOVERY INTERVAL

Now you rest, not sitting or standing still, but jiggling and walking about.

Your muscle-pumps idle and your bloodstream slows. But your heart-pump continues to beat at its full exercise pace for several seconds—maybe five, or fifty. This sets up a new relationship between the heart and the bloodstream. Each cardiac contraction must now work against a lazing blood flow that is losing momentum. So the heart muscle has to strain.

Its walls stretch a bit. Muscle fibers in the walls enlarge and lengthen a bit. This is your moment of truth, the birth of the so-called "training effect." Presently, your heart beat slackens and that particular training bout is over.

So runs the theory.

Interval Training is a form of exercise which uses that brief moment of "training" over and over. Its virtue is that it seems to provide greater improvement in less time than any other system. It does this by "teaching" the heart to accomplish more work per beat.

More work per beat is the name of the game. More work per beat is the secret of human endurance. The records of world-class athletes like Haag, Pirie, Kuts, and Zatopek are the result of IT. I wondered if IT would work for us ordinary Joes. Anecdotal evidence said it would.

An acquaintance of Dr. Gerschler told about an eighteen-year-old girl who had been through heart surgery. With Interval Training, she was brought back to strength in just twenty-one days.

A fellow member of the American College of Sports Medicine, Dr. Vojin Smodlaka, told me how he used IT to rehabilitate his cardiac patients. Trained in Yugoslavia, he had learned and applied Interval Training as sports physician for the Yugoslav Olympic team. When he emigrated to the United States, he used the work-and-rest principle on his bedfast patients and saw their hearts grow strong. A mounted bicycle wheel enabled them to pump with their hands instead of their feet. A friction device increased the work load according to their progress.

Sick people and unfit people have one thing in common: they are reluctant to start exercising. "It's too hard," they complain. Dr. Smodlaka started his patients with an easy thirty-second exercise period repeated three times. Ninety seconds of exercise. Old-timers scoffed, predicting failure. But the IT principle prevailed. Something happened to those hearts. They gradually got stronger, able to sustain heavier loads through more repetitions.

Despite Dr. Smodlaka's success, many cardiologists remained indifferent or skeptical. They were still hung up on the notion that exercise could injure the heart anew. "Aren't you afraid when you exercise a heart patient?" a doctor asked Smodlaka at a medical conference.

"I'm afraid when my patient is quiet," the doctor replied. "I am not afraid when my patient works."

Interval Training can take much of the work out of old-style exercising. Its work load can be adjusted to fit any individual's need. Returning from that world congress on sports medicine in Hanover, and after discussions with Dr. Smodlaka, I realized that I had a way of exercising that everyone could enjoy with a minimum of fatigue and discomfort—and I knew the "tool" for it was the jump rope.

# 3

# How Your Body Functions

The difference between the unfit person and the fit—to borrow from Mark Twain—is the difference between the lightning bug and the lightning.

It was Plato who said, "Lack of activity destroys the good condition of every human being, while movement and methodical exercise saves it and preserves it." Our nation is slowly accepting his view. Today thousands of physicians have begun to prescribe exercise.

Why do we age? Many scientists are studying the question, and one reason seems to be the pattern of stress that batters our nervous system. The old school of therapy sought to eliminate stress but found it impossible. Stress is life.

Stress is so many things: the seeking after security, the holding down of a job, or the simple desire to "be somebody." In particular, the housewife is beleaguered. Cooking, making beds, and cleaning house are said to be as heavy a load as work performed by a man in a plant. Add mothering and wifing and taxi service for the hubby who commutes, for the daughter who takes ballet lessons, for the son who plays Little League baseball . . .

Dr. Roger Revelle, director of Harvard's Center for Population Control, says that the American woman is "the loneliest, hardest-working woman who has ever lived."

My purpose in writing this book is to offer an escape, not from stress, but from the defeatism imposed by an unfit body. If medicine is something that cures, then exercise is a very powerful medicine. What exercise is and what exercise does are the message of this medium.

Facts about health-through-exercise are not as widely known as they should be. Most physicians have become specialists devoted to body parts (eye-ear-nose-throat, internal organs, skin), which makes sense when it allows a practitioner to become more expert. But it often lulls a patient into a false sense of security after his hurt is healed. Thinking he is well again (when only the disease, not its cause, has been cured), he returns to his former life-style and is stricken again.

The solution, of course, is to treat the whole body. Occasionally, a prominent physician will recognize this and spell it out. Which is why so many cheered several years ago when Dr. Edward L. Boortz, a former president of the American Medical Association, declared, "It begins to appear that exercise is the master conditioner for the healthy and the major therapy for the ill."

Exercise is a master conditioner because it restores the entire body, not merely a failing part. No pill, no hypodermic, no scalpel can make that claim. This, vastly simplified, is how it works.

### Skin:

Within its privacy, several major and minor systems form a partnership. The major systems are your bones, muscle, blood, nerves, glands, and digestive tract. The system that binds them all together is circulation.

Your circulation is a food-bearing river of blood and plasma which provides every cell in your body with good nutrition. The enrichment of this river depends on both glandular and digestive systems.

Skin is a system in itself. Its public face is constantly challenged by heat, cold, wind, and microbes. The latter are killed by chemicals that spew from invisible springs in your cuticle. Its outer cells roughen, thicken, turn dark, and die in a lifelong process of desquamation. Like shingles on an aging roof, they curl and spin away on the wind, and then, unlike a roof, new shingles appear spontaneously in the bare spaces.

Your skin's private side encloses a dark, aquatic world crowded with the wet tissues of your organs, muscle, and bones. Blood bathes them constantly—or until your movements become too timid to keep open the irrigation canals.

Flip Wilson was wrong when he said, "What you see is what you get." What strikes the eye may be tall, dark, and handsome, but inside your cuticle is where the action is.

**Blood:**

Your skin covers all, and your blood penetrates all. Blood is the most amazing solution known to man. Six times thicker than water, it teems with goodies, spurting from the heart's left ventricle into the master channel called the aorta, penny-bright with the sheen of pure oxygen, rushing like a millrace or tiptoeing along. Take a closer look.

Young blood was used by the ancients as a medicine. Louis XI of France drank the blood of several infants, but his disease persisted. A Pope drank the blood of several young men. He died.

Its redness comes from red cells called *erythrocytes*, which number 25,000 to 30,000 *billion* per human body. Somebody has figured out that if your red cells were placed side by side, they would stretch for 1,000 miles.

Blood's purity is guarded by invisible white cells called

*leukocytes*, about 50 million. White cells are scavengers that move in the bloodstream seeking out infiltrators. A drop of blood seen under a microscope reveals an incredible concourse of red and white cells, proteins, carbohydrates, fats, sugars, acids, minerals, and wisps of glandular secretions. And there are countless platelets, tiny sandbags that form dams and keep you from bleeding to death. These are so small, they say, that 250,000 could march simultaneously through the eye of a needle. Finally, there are sticky chemical shreds called fibrinogen which swim into wounds, where they turn into threads which make a net that catches passing platelets and converts them into the airtight plug we call a scab.

The bloodstream is also a transportation system, perhaps the most amazing on land or sea. Its length may be as much as 100,000 miles. Its primary function is to feed your body's hungry universe.

By counting the cells in a drop of blood, a scientist can assay the state of your health. If it's good, the count for red cells should be 4,500,000 to 5,000,000 per cubic centimeter. The count for white cells should be from 5,000 to 10,000. If infection attacks the body, the white count zooms to provide more germ fighters.

Blood travels far and fast through a plumbing network made up of arteries (big round, muscle-covered pipes) and arterioles (smaller muscle-covered pipes) and capillaries, which have a wall so thin that food seeps through in one direction while waste seeps through in the other to ride the bloodstream to kidneys and lungs. You are supposed to have 317,000,000 capillaries.

Your five or six quarts of blood circle through your body about fifteen hundred times each day. Activity raises the flow by as much as eight or ten times. Stop your circulation and you are in trouble. Four minutes without blood and the brain dies or is damaged forever.

Your blood picks up food and fuel from two important

supply depots. These are the small intestine and the lungs. In the former, powerful enzymes attack whatever your stomach has digested, turning meat and potatoes into amino acids, which are absorbed into undulating walls covered with a velvety nap that accepts the digested protein and carbohydrate and transfers it to the bloodstream.

Lungs clean the blood and revitalize it. Minuscule air sacs—650,000,000, they say—have walls so cobwebby that the body waste called lactic acid (now dissolved in your blood) can trickle into them, turning to carbon dioxide gas which can be exhaled.

As you inhale, air fills your lungs and the oxygen in that air seeps through air sac walls into your blood. Your red cells have a fantastic affinity for oxygen. As they tumble through your lungs they soak up oxygen like sponges. In a split second, once soiled and fatigued red corpuscles have perked up, squared their shoulders, and floated off in search of new adventures.

Red cells live a hard life. They grind their way through miles of tight arteries and veins, get hung up on calcified shoals, and bog down in atherosclerotic swamps. Look at a drop of blood through a microscope and they look like Raggedy Anns, their outlines often as lumpy as a pug's nose. They live an average of only a hundred and twenty days. Experts tell us that each second of your life, 10,000,000 red cells die. Fortunately, another legion is encamped and waiting. Their bivouac is in your bones.

**Bones:**

The size and shape of each individual's bones are largely inherited. They are the factories that manufacture the red and white blood cells.

You have over two hundred bones, almost all of them hinged to some other bone. They are 30 percent water, have twice the strength of oak wood, and pound for pound are stronger than steel.

Your bones and their marrow, penetrated by thousands of blood vessels and nerve filaments, are constantly at work creating new life. As old blood cells die, factories within the flat bones manufacture replacements. Let a police dog charge or a drunken driver sideswipe your car, your bones release reinforcements. In a crisis—and in exercise—your blood volume increases, and under ordinary conditions your entire blood supply is recreated every forty days.

But bone factories grow inefficient. Authorities call it old age. Physiologists call it lack of exercise.

**Muscles:**

You have over 650 muscles, each of which can lift 1,000 times its own weight. Stretch it and it springs back like a rubber band. Stimulate it electrically and it will shorten. This quality is what moves the world.

The three kinds of muscles are: striated muscle, smooth muscle, and heart muscle. "From birth to death, muscles play a critical role in everything we do. They propel us into the world in the first place—when the womb suddenly empties itself. They provide nearly all our internal heat. They push food along the digestive tract, suck air into lungs, and squeeze tears from lachrymal glands. And finis is written for us when the heart muscle, after beating two and one-half billion times in a seventy-year span, falters and fails."*

Some muscles tighten and relax constantly, squeezing blood through arteries and veins. "Smooth" muscles churn the intestines, facilitating digestion and evacuation. Muscles hold you together: for instance, the leg bones are joined at the knees by ligaments which are secured by muscles.

Muscles provide a sixth sense, a sense of "feel" that is more than touch. In the dark, you are handed a ball and you know at once that it is round. Dr. Arthur Steinhaus, Michigan State University physiologist, has said, "You can get along without

* J. D. Ratcliff, "The Miracle of Muscle," in *Today's Health* and *Reader's Digest*, May, 1956.

sight, sound, smell, and taste, but not without muscle sense. Without it, you couldn't even find your mouth."

Then there is also muscle *tone*. A flaccid muscle is useless. One with tone is always lightly tensed, ready to perform. Babies are born without muscle tone. By eight or nine years, most children have developed resting tone but not sitting or standing tone, which is why they slump in their chairs. Telling them to sit up does no good. Their slump will not improve until adolescence.

In adults, poor tone results in tiredness. The bones tilt; the abdomen sags; the head juts forward. We think of muscles as being essential for shoveling snow or carrying a three-year-old around the supermarket, but muscles are mainly needed for everyday tasks, such as sweeping, ironing, raking, pencil pushing, and standing up straight.

Strength and elasticity diminish with age. Only exercise maintains muscle tone. Without it, one drags through life. With good tone, one copes and occasionally capers.

A muscle is composed of billions of tiny cells. Take a fine hair about 1½ inches long—that is the size of the average muscle cell. The cells are wrapped into bundles, and these bundles are wrapped into larger bundles, all served with fresh blood, and with twigs of nerve fiber to make them contract. For a light load, only a few bundles are mobilized. When these tire, other bundles are switched on and the original worker-bundles rest. The heavier the load, the more bundles are activated, until a maximum is reached with all bundles committed.

The neglect is very obvious when certain muscles, such as the abdominal muscles, are not exercised. The abdominal cavity is a cage for your stomach, intestines, and a crowd of organs. Its floor is a bony pan called the pelvis. Its back wall of muscle is reinforced by your spine. Its roof is the heavy muscle called the diaphragm. The front wall is composed of tight, flat muscles kept in place by muscle tone.

When an active person becomes sedentary, his muscle tone (that slight tension) diminishes and the taut, three-way stretch of muscles across one's front turns into a three-way sag. What follows is like the first domino in a row that pushes over the next and the next. When the front wall sags, the intestines have more room. So they uncoil a bit, filling up the added space, and now they cannot push food along so efficiently. Thus waste products putter about and fall into intestinal folds and cul de sacs. Putrified gas bubbles through the loose gut, swelling it. The abdominal cage gives in only one direction—forward, so pressure from within stretches the weak abdominal muscles further and further.

And you've got a pot. God knows it's unsightly, but worse still, it is unhealthy. Organs work best when firmly packed into their muscular cage.

**Nerves:**

A single nerve cell consists typically of a polywog head *(neuron)* and a kite-tail filament from one inch to three feet long. The head is a small, charged-up storage battery that can send a tiny jolt of electricity the length of its tail at 200 miles per hour. With training, it can do this at a rate of five to ninety jolts per minute, like a machine gun that never needs reloading.

Every neuron has connections to other neurons which have connections with other neurons through cat-whisker processes called *dendrites*. Most neurons are located in the brain or the spinal column (making up the central nervous system). Their tails are often bound together like the wires of a coaxial cable. They penetrate every part of the body. If one could invent 10,000 American Telephone and Telegraph Companies, each with all kinds of switchboards and transistorized panels, their combined complexity would not equal that of the communications system of a single human being.

A muscle contracts only when a nerve tells it to. Some

nerves are commanded by the brain and some operate automatically. The automatic *(autonomic)* network stimulates your heart, controls your breathing, and moves your bowels.

The brain-directed nervous system requires an act of will, a mental calculation involving thousands of messages received via the body's sensors. These invisible "feelers" polka-dot every inch of your skin, muscle, and internal organs. Taste receptors (buds) in your tongue transmit signals which your brain organizes, and its printout says "too sweet" or "too sour." Our ears hear via 100,000 nerve ends which wave like wheat in the wind, as J. D. Ratcliff describes it, and this minuscule movement generates a feeble electric current. When it is amplified a thousand times, it is fed into the brain and recognized as a tone.

Much more complex are the eyes, which use 200,000,000 light receptors to record designs and colors and flash them to the brain in great sheets of technicolor information.

Skin sensors relay a warning when a skillet is dangerously hot. Others signal cold drafts and chilled feet. If the body temperature drops too much, the brain orders muscles to shiver, an activity designed to heat up the tissues.

Our blood supply, about six quarts, is circulated around our vascular system. Nerves operate this system.

Special feelers called *proprioceptors* are threaded into skeletal muscles for the purpose, it seems, of telling your brain about the body's position. Bike riders depend on proprioceptors to maintain their balance. So do you when you get up at night and walk through total blackness.

Several years ago, I attended a seminar conducted by Dr. Arthur Steinhaus, one of America's greatest physiologists. He tried to make the audience understand how our nervous system works.

"Picture your nerve impulses as burning their way through your bodies at an average speed of 150 miles per hour," he said. "They travel over strands resembling thin firecracker wicks which connect with the brain, running in and out and up and down and connecting muscles, skin, bones, and organs. Some connections are as regular and fixed as a trolley running straight through town. Others are as governed by chance as the path of an aimless driver."

He asked us to imagine a snow-covered town at dawn. Each impulse, like the wheels of a vehicle running through fresh snow, leaves a track, and wherever it crosses another track it makes a permanent connection. When a second impulse follows that same trail through those same connections, we are building a "rut" which we call a memory or perhaps a habit. When these "ruts" lead to admirable actions, we become known as persons of character. When they lead to criminal acts, we become known sometimes as jailbirds.

The Steinhaus picture ended: "The pavement and qualities of the street may be inherited, but how they are to be used is determined by the million-and-one forces of the environment which, playing upon the eyes, ears, and other senses, determines the course of the 'traffic.' "

Nerves can be conditioned through training to behave themselves even under extreme provocation. "Nerves of steel" are part of the coping equipment of the fit person.

Blood, bones, muscles, and nerves are only part of the extraordinary machinery of the human body. But an awareness of how they work makes clear how important their care and exercise is. It was Emerson who reminded his neglectful generation that the body is the mother of all inventions, a patent office in which every original model is stored, all the tools and engines on earth being only extensions of its limbs and its senses.

The personal experience of commanding your inherited power is as exciting as any scientific discovery. Your legs are not obsolete, nor is your heart a pale copy of its ancestors. To regain your legacy, you need only apply a one-word rule. In short, you need to *move*. Especially your legs.

Part Two

# YOUR PERSONAL SKIPPING PROGRAM

# 4

# Things You Need to Know

Now, as you are ready to begin your own training, here are answers to questions that probably are on your mind.

## THE ROPE

Sash cord, sizes 7 to 10, is satisfactory. It may be cotton, polyethylene, nylon. Some jumpers like a heavy cord, some a light one. (Ropes cost so little, you can afford to experiment.) It should be long enough to reach from armpit to armpit while passing under both feet. Tie a knot in or wrap a tape around each end. Sash cord is available in hardware stores. Sporting goods stores have good jump ropes with easy-turning handles. I have enjoyed using a rope made of an 8-ounce length of stretch cord with handles that fit together to provide a bonus of calisthenic and isometric exercises.

## WHO CAN SKIP?

Anyone who has exercised regularly can skip. Anyone who doesn't know how can easily learn by following the instructions on page 73. Persons over sixty years of age who have not exercised continuously should skip rope only after two conditions have been met. First, they should have consulted their doctor and passed a treadmill or bicycle stress test to determine the integrity of their hearts. Second, they should have built up their stamina over a period of time by less rigorous activities (such as walking or jogging) and our Rope Jumper's Test on page 61.

## WHERE TO SKIP

Anywhere is the best place—almost. Don't try it in a small room with low chandeliers or tall lamps. A flying rope can be as destructive as a bull in a china shop. Most kitchens are large enough, so are some bathrooms. I have used my carport, patio, porch, office, and basement. University students do it in dormitory hallways. Elementary school children do it in classroom aisles. Whole classes use the gymnasium or soccer field. Outdoors—take your pick of shady, cool spots.

## WHEN IS THE BEST TIME?

Some skippers like the early morning, and so do I. It's a wonderful way to wake up the body and stimulate the mind. Put it off and something always comes up. Three minutes minimum, with the heart rate up to your target rate (see page 95), and you're finished for the day.

Before any meal is a good time, too. Some people who are

overweight find that jumping before a meal reduces their appetite. After a meal, wait one to two hours, depending on the intensity of your workout. Experience is the best guide.

I know a physician who has substituted a bedtime skipping session for sleeping pills. After a workout and a tepid shower, he is so relaxed he falls asleep instantly.

## WHAT KIND OF CLOTHES?

Another reason why skipping is the perfect exercise is that you can wear any old clothes you want—or almost none. (I recommend at least a jockstrap for men and a bra for women.) Make yourself comfortable in loose-fitting garments. Slightly "potty" jumpers may find that a belt or some other support around the abdomen is helpful. One of my buxom acquaintances wears her husband's vest, tightly buttoned.

## THE INDIVIDUAL SESSION—HOW OFTEN?

Scores of research experiments have tried to provide a clean-cut answer to how often one must exercise. People are so different and conditions vary so much that we are not saying "positively," but if you are an average American male or female (age doesn't matter) then the consensus of scientific information today is that you will make maximum progress and achieve maximum fitness by exercising five or six times each week.

A German study by Dr. H. Roskamm, from the University Medical Clinic in Freiburg, has reported that thirty minutes of training five times a week produced a significant increase in the working capacity of younger persons, their improvement running from 10 to 20 percent. A multitude of other studies reach the same conclusion.

In a study by Dr. Michael L. Pollock of Lake Forest University, subjects who trained two days a week lowered their time for running two miles by only 48 seconds. But those who trained four days a week lowered theirs by 186 seconds.

Three times a week is also good, but the rate of improvement is slower.

Once maximum fitness is achieved, two exercise sessions per week are probably enough for maintenance.

One session a week is inadequate, and really useless as well as possibly harmful. Don't be a weekend athlete.

## THE INDIVIDUAL SESSION— HOW LONG, HOW LITTLE?

Someone has suggested that the question of how long we should exercise can be answered by observing animals and man in his natural state. Cave men spent many hours each day foraging for food, as animals do today. African bushmen hunt game from dawn to dusk. We civilized humans probably hunted like that for millions of years. As predators, we have bodies equipped to move eighteen hours a day. Surely, this is part of the answer.

## WARNING SIGNS AND ADMONITIONS

If you have been sedentary or only slightly active, you should be aware of signs which might indicate that you are overworking your heart. Such danger signs are:

Pale or clammy skin

Persistent shakiness lasting for more than ten minutes after exercise

Cramps in the legs

Blueing of the lips or around the fingernails
Headache, dizziness, light-headedness
Nausea or indigestion
Restlessness in bed the night after exercise
Pounding of the heart lasting more than five minutes after exercise
Uneven heartbeats

Any workout should consist ideally of three parts:

1. The warm-up
2. The work phase
3. The cool-out or warm-down

Experts insist that a sedentary person who is taking up exercise for the first time should never go directly into vigorous work.

All of us should consider the weather. If the temperature is high and the humidity low, exercise. If the temperature is low and the humidity high, exercise. But if both humidity and temperature are high—over eighty degrees—see a good movie.

From my own experience I have found that if you feel "tightness" or "fullness" or pain in the chest, you should slow down. If you feel pain in the arms, or neck or shoulders, stop exercising and walk about until the pain subsides. Next day, start your workout at a less arduous level. And tell your doctor.

For anyone over thirty years of age, the safest course is to get a medical examination before exercising. Ask your doctor to check your heart by taking an ECG, which means electrocardiogram. This is done routinely while the patient lies on a couch or table. But you should know how your heart will handle *hard* work. So ask for a *stress* ECG, which means that the doctor will attach wires to your chest and then record the heart's reaction while you ride a bicycle, walk on a treadmill, or climb stairsteps.

The stress ECG is not infallible, but it helps. If your doctor does not have this equipment, call your local hospital. Treadmills are being installed by the hundreds. They just might tell you an inside story that will save your life.

Be aware of pain. Lack of adequate circulation in the heart can drive an agonizing dagger into your chest. It can also cause a mere ache in your teeth, arm, jaw, or ear. Don't disregard it. Stop exercising at once but continue to walk about. At the first opportunity—and before you exercise again—consult your personal physician.

Become aware of your pulse. After a workout, the accelerated pulse beat will slow down. As you become fitter, it will slow down faster. One benchmark for persons under forty is that it should drop to 120 beats per minute (give or take a couple of beats) within three minutes following a vigorous workout. If it hangs up there for as much as ten minutes, check it out with your M.D.

Many physicians are too busy to keep up with fast-breaking news about exercise physiology. You might want to supplement their knowledge with this list of "contraindications to participation in exercise programs" as prepared and distributed to the profession by a blue-ribbon panel of authorities who met under the auspices of the South Carolina Medical Association.

They warned that the following responses during exercise should lead to medical review:

Any chest pain, or pain referred to teeth, arm, jaw or ear

Syncope (fainting), light-headedness, or dizziness following exercise

Irregular heart rate following exercise

Persistent fatigue

Unusual weight loss

Musculoskeletal problems aggravated by exercise

Nausea, vomiting, or a feeling of malaise

Failure of the pulse to recover below the 140-beats-per-minute area within five minutes after cessation of exercise.

# 5

# Five Tests for Fun and Fitness

We all want to know how good we are.

Our ego demands it and our safety recommends it. Physiologists have devised hundreds of tests to appraise human fitness. The first tests were mostly measures of strength—how much a man could lift or a horse could pull. Later, they measured endurance, counting the miles one could run or the speed of a sprint. Today's tests, for the most part, reflect the health of the heart itself.

Here are several quickies which are reasonably accurate and which are guaranteed to stimulate conversation during any dull social gathering.

But mostly they are fun to do because they provide a ballpark estimate of how good you are.

## HOW TO TEST YOUR PULSE

First you must know how to take your pulse. If you can do

this, you can guide yourself through a safe and efficient conditioning course.

Most people have learned to find their pulse and to count its beat, but if you have not learned, follow these steps.

1. Rest your forearm, palm up, on your lap or on a table.
2. Place the first three fingers of your opposite hand lightly on the surface of your wrist about 1½ inches from the base of the thumb, and ¾ inch from top of the wrist. Small veins can usually be seen under the skin's surface, but these are not what you want, as they carry no pulse beat. An artery at a lower depth carries blood directly from your heart.

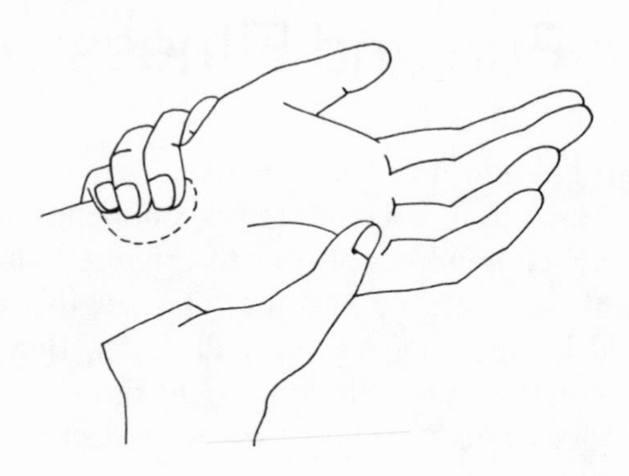

3. Press your fingers gently into the groove between the sinews in the middle of your wrist and the bone at its outer edge. Shift about a bit, if necessary, until you detect the rhythmic swelling of your invisible heartbeat.

Some people have trouble with this procedure. One remedy is to stand up and jog in place for fifteen seconds, which makes the beat stronger. After exercise, a convenient place to find your pulse is at the carotid artery in the side of the neck.

Raise your fingers to where the jawbone joins the neck below the ear. Press gently, moving straight down an inch or two, and you will feel the pulse beat. If the exercise has been rigorous, just lay your hand over your heart.

Most normal hearts beat, when subjects are sitting, from 72 to 80 times per minute. Some normal hearts beat as few as 50 times and others nearly 100 times a minute. Usually only the high rate is a cause for concern, suggesting a visit to your doctor.

## ORTHOSTATIC HEART STRENGTH

*Orthostatic* means pertaining to or caused by standing erect. When you lie down, the heart's work is easier. Your organs are all on the same level and the blood flows effortlessly through horizontal arteries and veins.

When you stand up, the heart works harder, for the bloodstream must be driven upward to serve the brain, and through a half-dozen up-and-down circuits serving organs and muscles. This added work load is reflected in the extra speed of the heartbeat. A strong heart takes the change of position with a modest increase in activity; a weak heart struggles and beats much faster. For years, specialists have compared resting and standing heart rates to measure cardiac efficiency.

To take the test:

1. Lie down for several minutes, long enough to give the heart time to slow down to its resting rate. Then count your pulse for one minute.
2. Stand erect (rising comfortably and without hurry) for sixty seconds and then count your pulse for one minute.
3. Note the difference between your resting rate and your standing rate. This difference registers your heart's ability to adjust. One study shows that average subjects have a resting rate of 74 beats per minute. When standing, the

same subjects average 92 beats per minute. The average increase for trained athletes is from 6 to 10 beats. Your difference should never be greater than 18 or 20 beats per minute.

## A TEST FOR RECOVERY FROM EFFORT

1. Take your pulse, sitting.
2. Climb a flight of stairs.
3. Take your pulse again.

If your heart is fit, your pulse after climbing the stairs will be around 88 to 90 beats per minute. If you're out of shape, it can zoom to 160. Anything over 90 needs improvement.

## A QUICK RECOVERY TEST

1. Take your pulse, sitting, to determine your normal heart rate.
2. Run in place for fifteen seconds.
3. Sit down and take your pulse, noting how long it takes to return to normal.

If it is back to normal in 30 seconds—EXCELLENT:
. . . 60 seconds—GOOD
. . . 120 seconds—FAIR
. . . from 120 to 189 seconds—POOR
If your heart rate is slower after exercise, tell your doctor.

## JOG-IN-PLACE TEST

A popular test used at the Cleveland YMCA requires a one-minute period of jogging. It's probably as accurate as any short test can be.

1. Run in place briskly for one minute.
2. Stop, sit, and take your pulse for fifteen seconds. Multiply by four to get your pulse rate per minute.

Your rating:

| | |
|---|---|
| 84 to 96 beats per minute | VERY GOOD |
| 102 to 114 | ABOVE AVERAGE |
| 120 to 132 | AVERAGE |
| 138 to 149 | BELOW AVERAGE |
| 150 to 161 | POOR |
| 162 and up | VERY POOR |

We have used the term "resting heart rate." This is the speed your heart beats when you are *sitting* at rest. When I awake in the morning, my heart rate is in the fifties. When I have eaten breakfast it rises into the sixties (sending blood to help my digestion). When I type and rise from time to time to consult reference works, it settles down to an average 72 beats per minute. When I skip rope, it rises to 120.

To use your pulse rate as a kind of exercise thermostat, you need to know:

1. Your resting heart rate (sitting)
2. Your maximum heart rate
3. Your heart reserve—which is the difference between the resting rate and the maximum rate.

Let's play that again. Your resting rate has been explained and understood, I trust.

Your *maximum* rate is something else. It is the number of times that your heart can pump per minute with the most severe exercises you can give it. Chase a bank robber until you drop or flee from a rapist until your legs turn to jelly—your heart will be trip-hammering in your chest at a speed approaching your maximum. This is nature's way of trying to provide all the oxygen your muscles need to meet the crisis; but all engines have a limit, even such a miraculous engine as your heart. That limit is your maximum heart rate. Chances are, you have never hit it. Nor is it necessary.

It is not necessary because Swedish studies have established the fact that the maximum rate declines with age at the rate of about one beat per year. Their tables, based on thousands of observations, will give you an approximation of your personal maximum according to your age and you don't have to lift a finger. Just refer to the table on p. 60.

Now, knowing your maximum (from the table), you deduct your resting rate, and the difference is your *heart reserve*, or the range in which your heart can pump effectively. Remember that the slower it pumps to deliver the oxygen your tissues need, the less fatigue you are apt to experience.

Let's take a forty-five-year-old man with a resting rate of 70. The table shows that his maximum rate is 180. His reserve area, therefore, is 180 minus 70 (resting rate), or 110.

Somewhere between 70 and 180 beats per minute is the level at which exercise causes the heart to adapt to a heavier load and to pump more blood, with less work. Many experiments have sought to ascertain exactly where this improvement begins. Does it start at 50 percent of your maximum? Or at 80 percent? Nobody knows for sure, but a rough consensus is available. Experts agree that there is little benefit to any exercise that does not drive the heart up to more than half of the extra beats per minute available between your resting rate and your maximum. In our example, our forty-five-year-old man had a reserve of 110. Fifty percent is 55. By adding 55 to his resting rate of 70, we get 125 beats per minute.

And that's it! That man's heart begins to improve when it beats more than 125 times a minute. That is the lower boundary of his success zone.

Now that we know where improvement begins, two questions arise. First, if a heart beats faster than 50 percent of its reserve, will it improve faster? The answer seems to be *yes*. Our forty-five-year-old will become fitter faster by exercising his heart at 140 beats per minute. And still faster at 150.

Second, if the beat rises to 160 or 170 beats per minute—is there a point where a prudent person should stop? Again, the answer is *yes*.

Scientists have exercised thousands of subjects at 70, 80, and even 90 percent of their maximum heart rates. If the principles of exercise regarding warm-up, progressive overload, and tapering off are observed, these levels are safe for any sound heart. Certainly an older person or an obese one should not attempt immediately to drive his heart up to anywhere near his maximum rate. But those levels, experiments have shown, are perfectly safe for college students and young fathers and mothers. To be doubly safe, however, many physical directors advocate a success zone around 65 percent of maximum for three months, then 75 percent of maximum for the next three months, and if no signs of distress appear, 85 percent of maximum as long as the program is maintained regularly.

If you are sedentary or only slightly active and aged thirty to thirty-nine, you should skip until your heart is beating around 123 times per minute. If you are forty to forty-nine, your target is lower, at 117. The chart on page 95 gives target rates for other ages and degrees of fitness.

Remember to take it easy. Train, don't strain!

You are unique, with your own unique capacity. If your heart beats a little slower or a little faster than the target figure, don't worry. As long as you keep it in the right neighborhood, you'll do all right.

TABLE A

HEART RATE DECLINE BY YEARS*

THE DECLINE OF "MAXIMUM" HEART RATE WITH AGE
POSSIBLE APPLICATIONS TO EXERCISE TESTING AND TRAINING

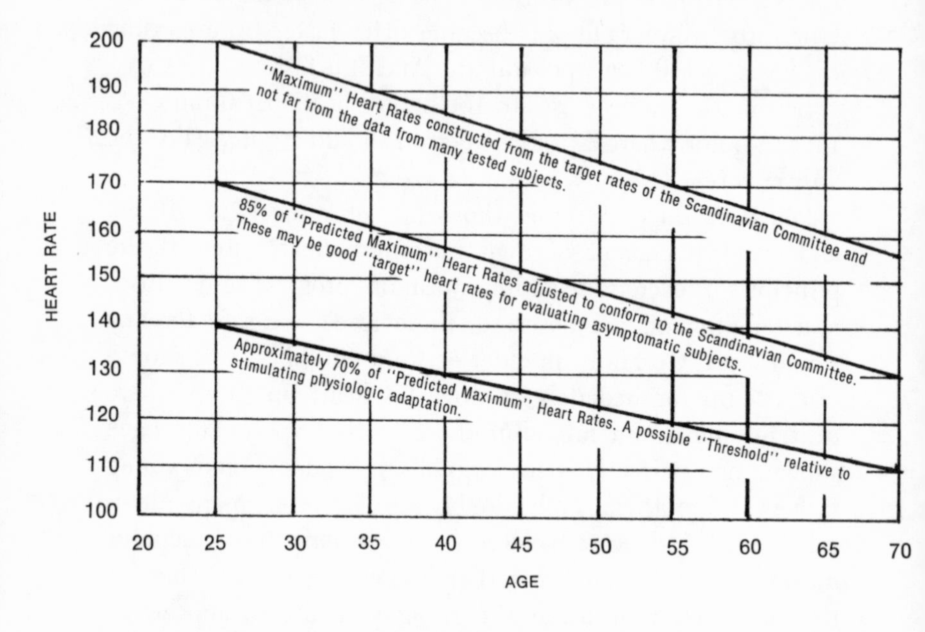


Top line indicates the maximum rate for various ages.

Middle line indicates a rate-for-age at which good training takes place.

Bottom line indicates a safe rate-for-age for testing organically sound but sedentary hearts.

* Chart taken from *Guidelines for Successful Jogging*, copyright © 1970, The National Jogging Association, Washington, D.C.

## THE ROPE JUMPER'S TEST

Some exercise physiologists dislike tests which grade a person against an average score. They say that people are unique and cannot be compared with each other. Also, a low score often discourages the very persons who need exercise the most.

These experts believe that the only meaningful grade is one reflecting personal progress. So here is a special test that reflects *you.* Use it periodically to measure your personal progress. It consists of a series of exercises, each separated by ten-second rest periods.

1. Skip for ten seconds.
2. Rest for ten seconds.
3. Skip for ten seconds.
4. Rest for ten seconds.
5. Skip and rest until you have completed ten sets of skipping and resting (total: one hundred seconds of exercise).
6. Sit down comfortably for fifteen seconds and then count your pulse for a full minute.
7. Your pulse count for that minute is your Starting Fitness Level. Don't compare it with anybody else's or any scale. This count is you. It's where you start. From now on, your objective is to get that count down—but slowly.

Repeat the test periodically. Keep a record.

Don't expect a big improvement right away. Somebody has estimated that for every year you have spent getting *unfit,* you must spend at least a month to regain fitness. The older you are, the longer it takes. But think of it this way—you can correct twenty years of abuse to your body with only twenty months of repair work.

# 6

# Getting Fit to Skip

If you are under thirty, you are probably limber and strong enough to go right into our skipping program (page 83).

If you are over thirty or suspect that a few days of limbering exercises will be helpful, I recommend these preliminary activities.

Do them for two weeks or so—they will loosen your joints, stretch your muscles, and make skipping easier. We'll start at the top and work down.

### THE NECK

1. Roll the head forward until your chin rests close to or on your chest, then raise the head and roll it

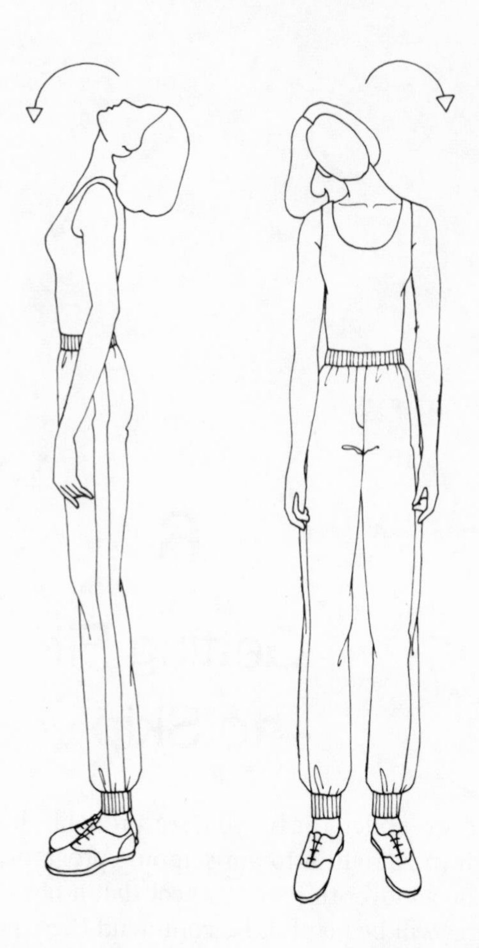

backward as far as it will go. Do this slowly, not forcing it. Five times.

2. Roll the head toward the right shoulder until it nearly touches. Then roll it straight over to the left shoulder. Five times.

3. Roll the head forward until you feel strain in the back of the neck, then slowly make it describe a clockwise circle toward and over the right shoulder, then back and across from right to left to the left shoulder, and on to the starting position. Twice. Do two circles in the opposite direction.

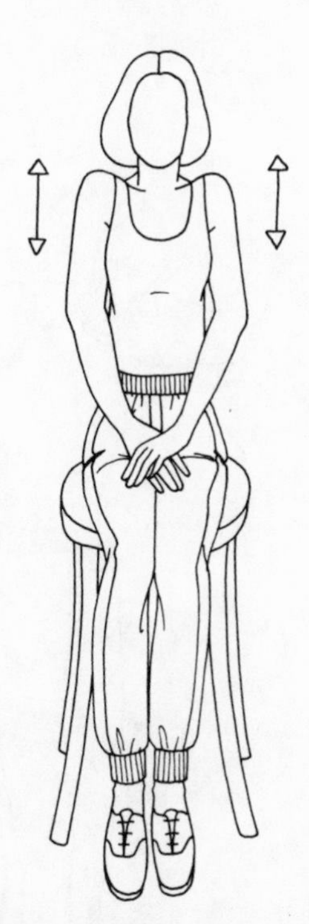

SHOULDERS

1. Sit erect in a straight chair, hands on thighs, with backbone away from back of chair. Raise shoulders toward ears as far as you can, then drop them. Three times.

2. Roll both shoulders straight forward, then relax and return to starting position. Three times.

3. Roll both shoulders back, trying to make your shoulder blades kiss. Relax and return to starting position. Three times.

4. Raise both shoulders and make their points describe a circle: forward and down, back and up and over—twice. Reverse the circle twice.

NOTE:
(If you are uncomfortable because of positioning the hands on the thighs, let them swing free. The important thing is to free up the shoulder muscles.)

SHOULDER SOCKET

1. Stand erect. Lean forward slightly and swing extended arms as if doing a fast overhand crawl. Lift them high out of the water. Ten times.

2. Straighten up and reverse the arms, imitating a backstroke. Keep the arms extended and let them flail away. Ten times.

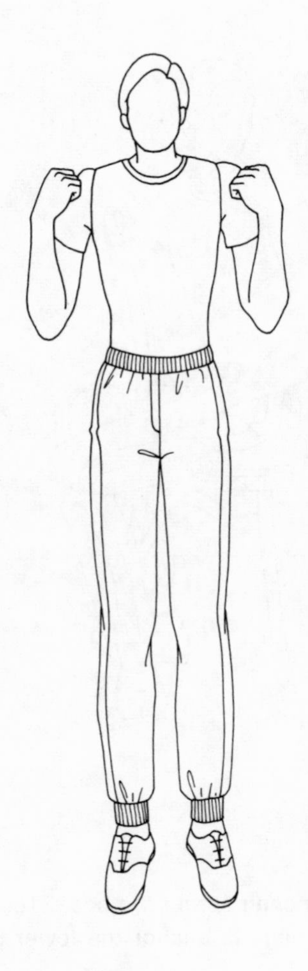

ELBOWS

Sit or stand. Extend arms straight forward and level, palms up. Make two fists. Bend the elbows sharply and strike yourself gently on the shoulders, and return to starting position. Five times.

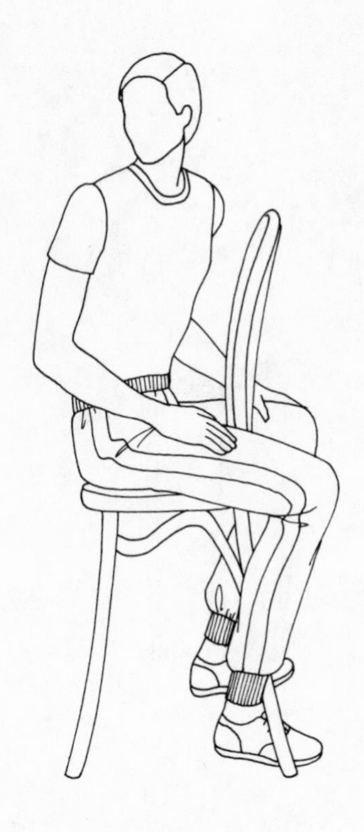

SPINE

1. Sit on a straight chair *facing the back.* Tuck your feet around the chair legs to anchor the lower part of your body.

a. Turn your upper body to the right, twisting at the waist. Pretend a mirror is directly behind you and you are trying to turn far enough to look into it. Do not force it.

Return to starting position. Repeat up to six times if you feel comfortable.

b. Repeat, turning to the other side.

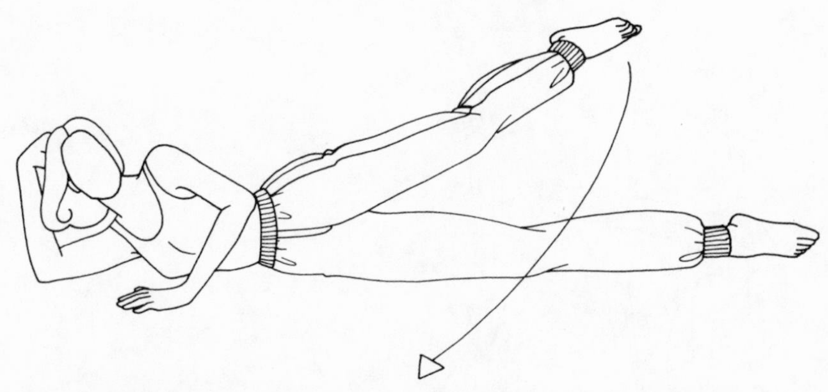

HIP JOINTS

1. Lie on your back on floor or hard mattress.

a. Roll onto your right side. Extend upper leg (left) as far forward as it will go. Then swing it backward across the other leg as far behind you as it will go. Return to starting position. Three times.

b. Lift upper leg straight toward ceiling and let it down slowly. Three times.

c. Turn on opposite side and repeat above with the other leg.

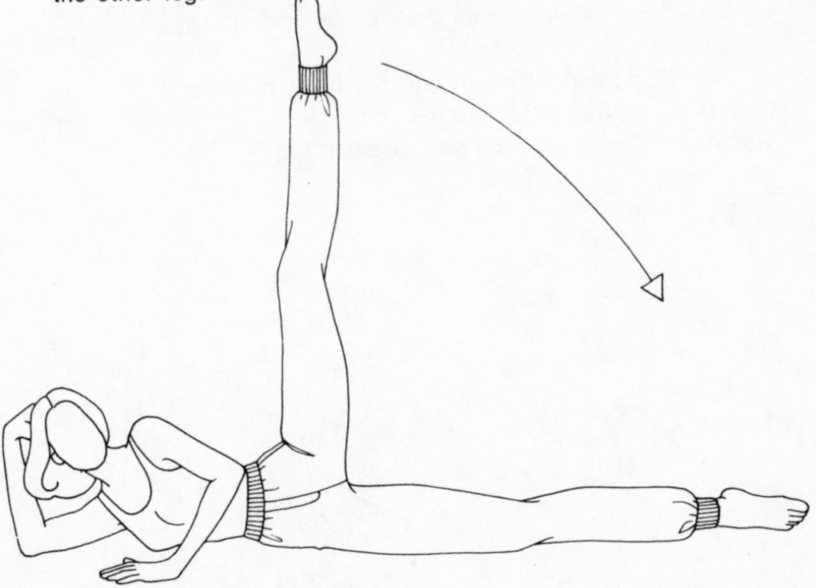

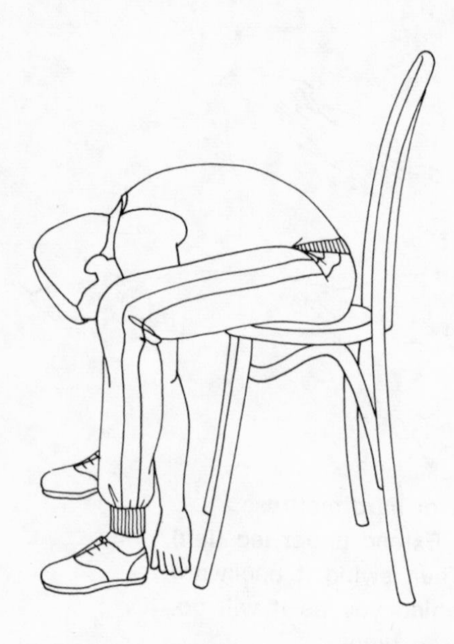

2. Sit on front edge of a bench or straight chair. Spread the knees.

a. Bend the body forward as far as you can.

b. Bob up and down gently several times.

c. Move your arms outside your knees and grasp your ankles.

d. Pull your torso gently toward the floor, bobbing the kinks out of your tight muscles.

Return to starting position and repeat twice.

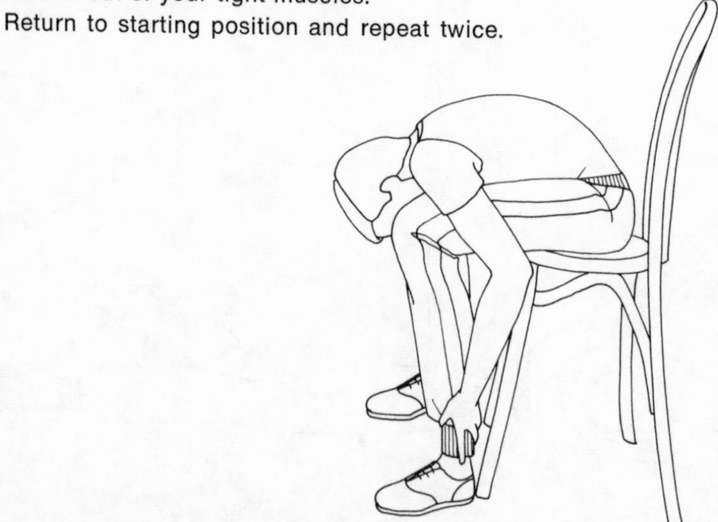

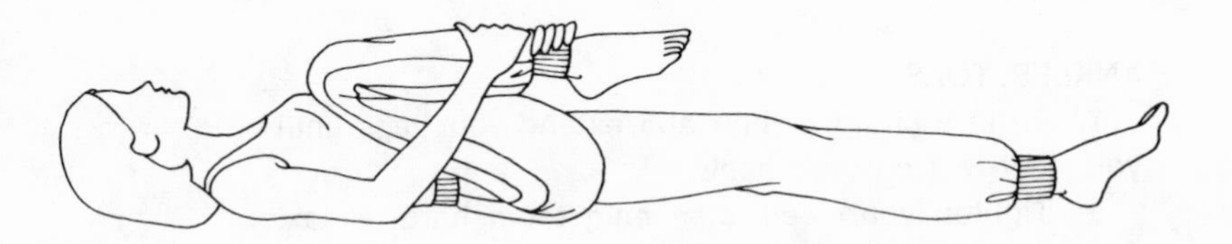

KNEES

1. Lie on back on floor or bed.

a. Raise right knee, leg bent, toward the chest.

b. Grasp lower leg with both hands and pull it gently until it touches the body. Five times.

c. Repeat with other leg.

2. Stand erect with your side to a sturdy table or chair. Grasp the piece of furniture with one hand to insure your balance.

a. Lift your outside foot backward, bending outside leg at the knee, until your foot is raised close to your hamstring muscle (back of thigh.)

b. Lean forward slightly in order to grasp your raised foot in your free hand.

c. Straighten up and draw the foot in to your hamstring until you feel a stretching sensation in the knee. Two times on each side.

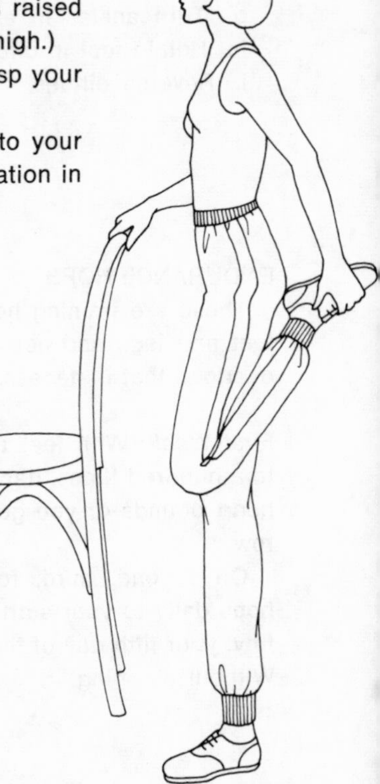

ANKLES, TOES

1. Sit in a straight chair and extend your legs until your feet rest on their heels.

a. Tighten your toes, clenching them hard. Relax. Repeat five times.

b. Stretch the toes, extending them, turning them up and back. Relax. Five times.

c. Raise the feet an inch or two off the floor. Straighten both ankles out and down as far as you can.

d. Bend the toes toward the knees, feeling tension in ankles and calves.

e. Turn the toes inward, pigeon-style; curl your soles toward each other.

f. Turn your feet out, like a skater with weak ankles, raising outside edges of both soles.

g. Turn ankles in and out, in and out, ten times.

h. Rotate feet in circles. Ten times.

i. Reverse circles. Ten times.

ENDURANCE HOPS

These are training hops intended to accustom your feet and legs and nerves to the continuous, rhythmic overload that is necessary to develop endurance.

*First Week:* With feet together, hop on both feet fifty to a hundred times, depending on how you feel. If your heart pounds or you get out of breath, do less tomorrow.

On second, third, fourth, and fifth days, add ten hops daily to your starting number. If you started with fifty, your fifth day of the week should see ninety hops. Without stopping.

*Second Week:* Start your second week of exercise with gentle hops plus the foregoing calisthenics and stretching movements. After warming up, change from hopping with both feet to running in place like a jogger. Start with a hundred steps, raising the feet about two inches, and adding ten steps each day until, on the fifth day, you are doing a hundred and forty.

Our intent is to correct the stiffening and hardening that your tissues have suffered over the years. Muscles and bones lose calcium if not used. Tendons tend to dry out. A muscle that is never stretched shortens, and fast or spurty movements can tear it. A common injury among beginning joggers is "jogger's heel." Mine once ached for six months because I had failed to prepare them for the impact of running on asphalt.

Jumping rope stresses the foot almost as much. The older the foot, the more care it needs. A soft surface is better than a hard one. Skip on a rug or mat, or wear shoes with a thick rubber sole. Old football knees are sometimes a problem. But treat your joints with care for the first two weeks of your program and they will return the favor with interest.

## IF YOU HAVEN'T SKIPPED BEFORE

Jumping rope is like swimming or riding a bike. Once learned, it is never forgotten. But what if you never learned?

First, learn to twirl the rope.

Second, learn to hop in rhythm.

Third, put the two together.

The entire process is so simple that toddlers can do it. For adults who insist on thinking for themselves (and most do), we offer these aids.

You will learn to do three kinds of hops:

1. The two-footed hop with rebound (see page 78).
2. The two-footed hop without rebound, also called "pepper" (see page 79).
3. The single-foot hop, or running skip (done with the rope turning at either half-speed or regular speed—see below and page 80).

You can hop profitably at either of two rhythms:

1. A slow turning of the rope (half-speed) while the legs make two hops (or a hop and a rebound, which is the same thing). This speed averages about 60 to 70 turns per minute.
2. A faster turning of the rope, with the legs taking one step per turn—usually about 140 to 160 turns per minute.

## Phase One: Learning to Twirl the Rope.

Stand in your skipping area and place both ends of your rope (or both handles) in the same hand. Position your hand approximately at hip level. The loop should touch the floor beside your feet. Your objective is to whirl the doubled rope in a vertical circle at your side. Grasping the ends firmly, move your arm and hand so as to lift the loop off the floor and swing it into a fore-and-aft arc that moves the loop from behind to above your head, and down in front. Keep it turning for a dozen or so twirls. As soon as the movement becomes comfortable, stop, switch the ends or handles to the other hand, and repeat.

**Phase Two: Learning to Hop in Time with the Rope.**

When you feel comfortable with phase one you are ready to learn to hop in time with the rope's rhythm. Not over the rope, just alongside it.

Twirl your rope again into an up-and-down circle and listen to its sound as the end of the loop strikes the floor. Get the feel of whirling it and hearing it. Change hands and repeat the routine.

Now twirl the rope and make a small hop, on both feet, each time it strikes the floor. Practice this until your hops are timed exactly with the rope sounds. Stop and change hands and continue to practice, letting the nerves of your arms and legs synchronize their signals, forming the habit ruts which will soon make jumping rope easy and pleasant.

**Phase Three: Putting Phases One and Two Together.**

Hold a rope handle or end in each hand, with the loop resting on the floor behind your feet. With the wrist motions you have just learned, swing the loop up over your head and down in front. As it strikes the floor in front of your feet (or maybe a split second earlier), hop just high enough for the rope to pass beneath your toes. Don't waste your energy on lofty, kangaroo-type hops. And don't expect to master the trick at the first attempt. It may be that your brain will soon be overwhelmed by self-doubt and discouragement. Hang in there. Your body is smarter than your brain: every move you make is a learning experience. Give your nervous system a chance and soon your muscles will be singing.

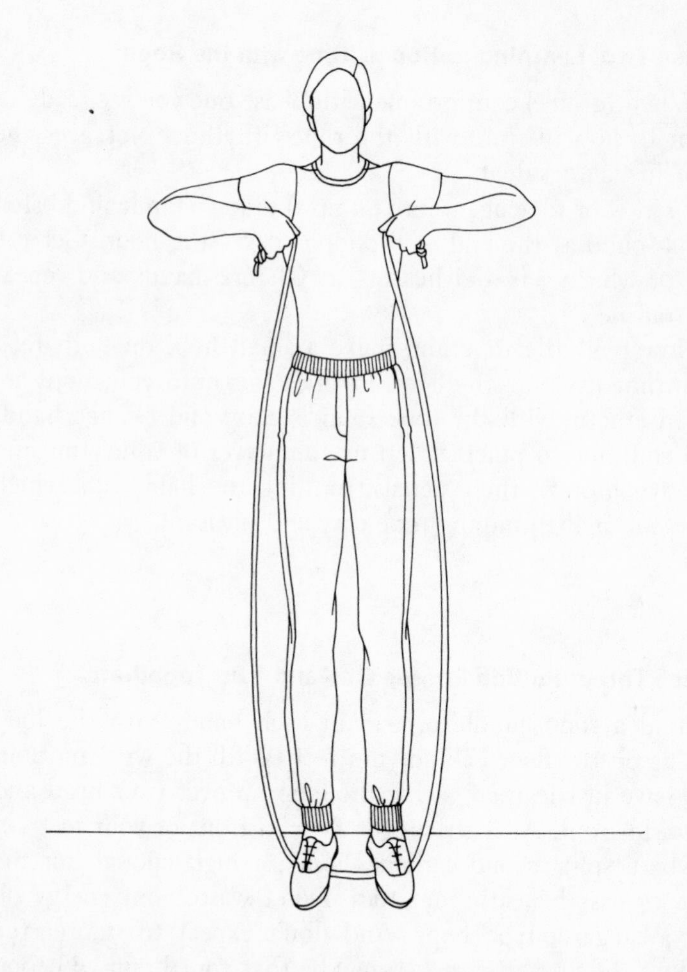

The length of your jump rope will vary according to your height. To find the right length for you, stand on the rope and draw its ends up to your armpits. Avoid jumping with a short rope. It is needlessly tiring.

## ONE-HANDED WHIRL

Place both ends of the rope (or both handles) in the same hand. Whirl the rope from back to front so it circles parallel to your side. Let the loop hit the floor lightly. The hand should make a circle 6 or 8 inches in diameter. For this exercise, just try to master whirling the rope. Change hands and do it again. Fifty turns or so on each side.

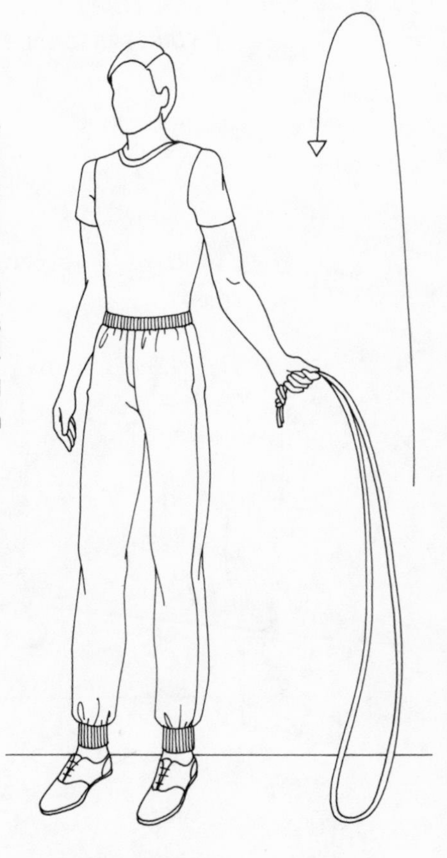

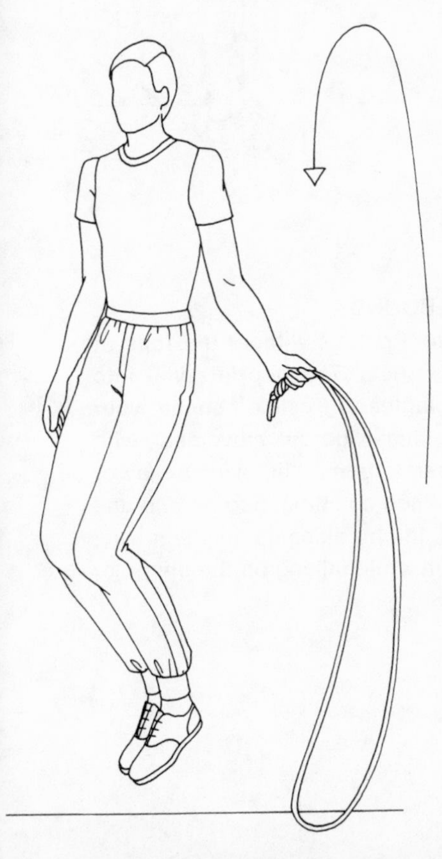

## ONE-HANDED WHIRL AND HOP

This exercise is to develop coordination between hand/eye/leg muscles. Whirl the rope from back to front for several turns, listening to the rhythm of it striking the floor. Begin to hop in time with its rhythm. Do five or six turns and rest. Change hands and repeat. When you are comfortable with two-footed hops, try running in place (a slow jog) while turning the rope.

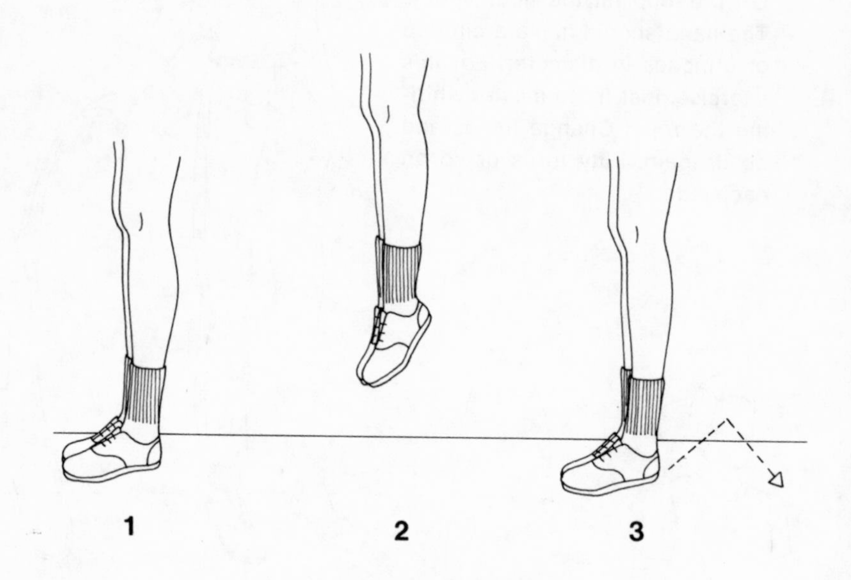


THE TWO-FOOTED HOP WITH REBOUND

This is the way most skippers begin. Practice without the rope at first. Counting *one-two-one-two* may help. The hop lifts you into the air high enough for the rope (imaginary) to slide beneath your feet. The rebound is an identical but less vigorous movement, with the knees flexing and the feet cooperating in a "lift" which may or may not take the feet off the floor. When counting, hop on *one* and rebound on *two*. This is so good for breaking in the legs and ankles that some skippers practice it while talking on the phone or waiting at check-out counters.

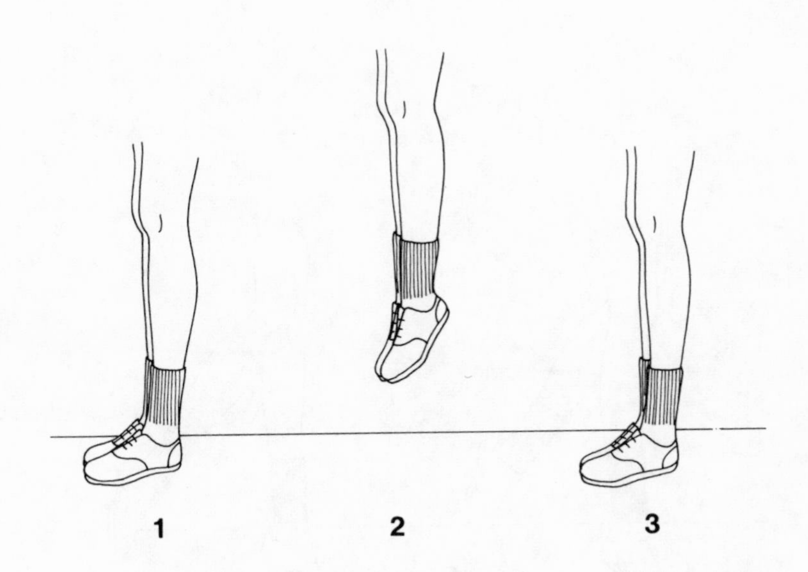


THE TWO-FOOTED HOP *WITHOUT* REBOUND

This step differs from the hop-with-rebound in that it is a continuous series of hops, each one high enough off the floor to clear the rope (when you use it). Practice a series of slow hops to increase your leg power and coordination. Practice fast hops (as fast as you can go) to increase your endurance and shed fat cells. When you start using a rope, you will do the hop-with-rebound while the rope is turning at half-speed. The hop-without-rebound will be done with the rope turning at whatever speed you choose, using one hop per turn. Learn both steps now, for they will be useful later in several exciting routines. (See Chapter 9.)

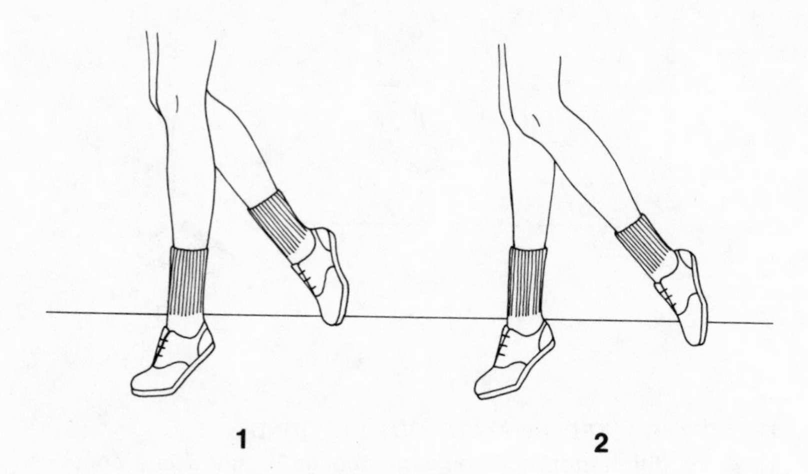


THE SINGLE-FOOT HOP
This step is exactly like running in place, only the feet are lifted a little higher as you jump from foot to foot. Also called the running skip, this is the standard step for all conditioning work. It usually raises the heartbeat about 5 or 10 extra beats a minute over the two-footed hop. Learn to do this at both rope speeds: i.e., half-time—taking two steps for each rope turn—and regular time—taking one step for each rope turn.

STARTING POSITION

If you start right, you will skip right. The rope's loop lies behind your heels on the floor. Your hands hold the ends lightly. Extend your arms forward. Execute the first turn with a hard down-and-back rotation of the extended arms. As the rope rises, bring your hands toward the hips and make small, vigorous circles with the hands. This movement is pure "feel," so don't be discouraged if you fail the first few times.

A STANDARD HOP

Once you have made the first turn, drop the elbows closer to the sides, but with room for free movement. The forearms relax and slope downward from the elbows so the hands are about 6 inches in front of your hip bones. For the first few sessions, hop a few times and rest. Get the feel of your rope (each one is different) and learn the knack of making a "soft" landing after every hop.

# 7

# The Famous Rodahl Skipping Program

You have practiced hopping and jumping and limbering for two weeks or so now, and you also know how to twirl a jump rope.

This week you settle down to a regular routine. It is based on procedures which have succeeded in the United States and Europe. In an earlier chapter, you read of the research conducted among workers at the Lankenau Hospital in Philadelphia by Dr. Kaare Rodahl. Afterward he returned to his native Norway to become director of the Institute of Work Physiology in Oslo, where he verified his earlier findings and published them in his book *Be Fit for Life* (New York: Harper & Row, 1966).

"To build and maintain fitness requires very little time and effort," he said, ". . . less than ten minutes a day five days a week."

Hereunder are the essentials of the program he "built around the skip rope." It is his opinion that "nothing surpasses the simple skip rope in producing the greatest fitness in the least amount of time."

First, warm up your body with one minute of slow skipping or running in place.

Rest for a half-minute.

Start your workout by skipping at a fairly fast rate and continue until you are out of breath.

Rest again.

Skip again until out of breath.

Your exercise format from now on will vary only a little. As a rule, you will skip vigorously, then rest, over and over, five days each week. Gradually your heart will become stronger and your endurance longer so that your exercise bouts will expand and your rest periods will contract. Your long range goal is to do 500 rope turns in succession without missing—all in five minutes. When you can do that, you will be as fit as you need to be. As your program continues, you will be taught new steps and routines, or you can invent some of your own.

When you skip, relax. Look straight ahead. Jump just high enough—about an inch—for the rope to pass under your feet.

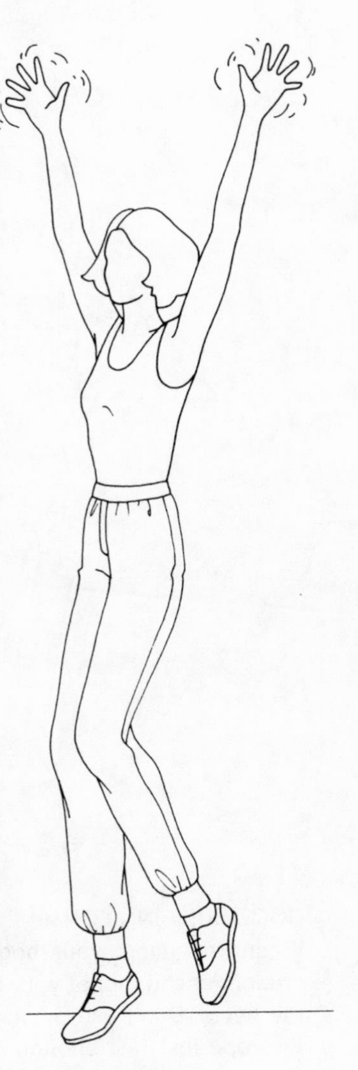

THE WARM-UP

The warm-up is of the utmost importance, especially as you become more expert and skip with more vigor. It is not necessary to use your rope during warm-up. Merely hop about from foot to foot, or do two-footed hops. Trot around your skipping quarters; rise high on your toes for a dozen steps; bend your knees in a "Groucho Marx" walk. Raise your arms overhead for a half-dozen steps, shaking and vibrating them. Then drop them to your sides and let them hang loose. Shake the hands vigorously. And stay relaxed.

GOOD JUMPING FORM

When you jump, your body should be erect but relaxed. Look straight ahead, not at your feet. Land on the balls of your feet, not the heels. Don't use much arm movement. In the beginning, turn the rope just fast enough to keep it in its arc. As you gain confidence, you can speed up. Jump on a soft surface or wear thick-soled shoes.

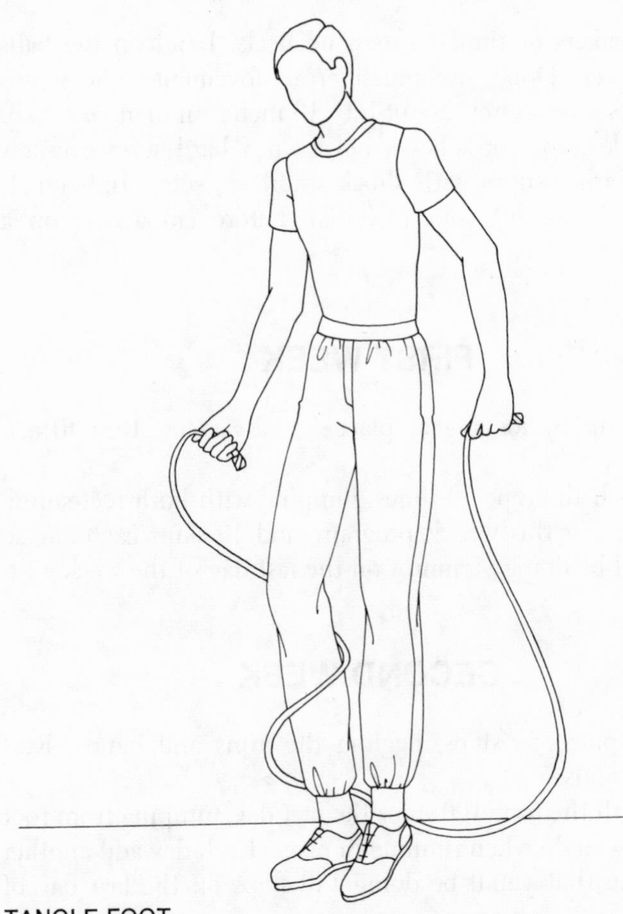

TANGLE FOOT

Expect to have dozens and maybe hundreds of tangles. Some days, you'll learn, will be worse than others. It's in your nervous system and your coordination, but with practice all systems will learn to go together. When you encounter a "Tangle Foot," don't panic and jump about, trying to maintain your rhythm, which most jumpers do instinctively. Instead, extricate your feet and legs, arrange the loop behind your heels, breathe deeply, and start all over. If you are in the midst of a numbered sequence (working up to 100 turns, for instance), resume where your counting broke down and continue to your objective.

Wear sneakers or similar shoes, no heels. Land on the balls of your feet. Don't use much arm movement. The hands should describe a circle about 8 to 10 inches in diameter. Skip on a thick carpet or a lawn, never on a hard surface unless you're wearing shoes with shock-absorbing soles. Individuals over forty: Consult your physician before embarking on a program.

## FIRST WEEK

Warm up by jogging in place 50 easy steps. Rest fifteen seconds.

Skip with the rope 50 times, jumping with both feet simultaneously. For this week's program, add 10 skips each day so that you'll be doing 90 jumps on the last day of the week.

## SECOND WEEK

Jog in place 50 steps, jiggling the arms and hands. Rest fifteen seconds.

Skip with the rope 100 steps the first day, jumping from foot to foot as you do when running in place. Each day add another 10 skips so that you'll be doing 140 skips on the last day of the week.

## THIRD WEEK

Warm up with 50 jogging steps.

Perform 100 skips without stopping, stepping over the rope as if running in place. Rest for fifteen to thirty seconds (or more if you are breathing hard and your heart is pounding). Skip 100 more steps without stopping.

NOTE: It is inevitable that your clumsy feet will get tangled up in your rope. Don't panic or waste energy trying to recover. Just resume skipping as soon as you can and continue on until you have performed the prescribed number of steps.

## FOURTH AND SUBSEQUENT WEEKS

The goal from here on is to increase the number of skips in each skipping round or inning. Last week you did two rounds of 100 steps each. As your stamina improves, try to make each sequence longer. Every day add a few more skips to yesterday's record. Your objective, as was stated, is to achieve a fitness level that will enable you to perform 500 skips in succession. Remember always to observe the principle of progressive overload. That means you must get out of breath. Anything less *does not result in any appreciable training effect.*

## ADVANCED SKIPPING—ANY WEEK

### Warm-up:

Run in place 100 steps, bouncing at least 4 inches off the floor and lifting the knees high. Rest fifteen seconds. Follow up with 100 straddle hops—bouncing off both feet simultaneously and landing with your feet about 18 inches apart, then bouncing again to return to starting position.

### Workout:

Skip 200 times without stopping. Each successive day, add 10 skips to your workout until you reach your goal of 500 continuous steps. In thirty days (or six weeks at five times per week) you'll be celebrating.

## FOR SUPER-SKIPPERS

When you can skip 500 times without difficulty, you are ready for double-dip skipping. These are skips when you jump once (both feet together) but your rope revolves around your body *twice*.

**Warm-up:**

Repeat the warm-up for advanced skipping.

**Workout:**

Do a series of 200 continuous skips. Instead of stopping, continue with another series of 100 in which every third skip is a "special," jumping high enough to allow the rope to whirl under you *twice* before you come down to earth, as on p. 130. To repeat, in this sequence you do two standard skips, then a double-turn, two more standard skips, another double-turn, continuing through the series of 100 skips.

This last maneuver is really vigorous exercise, but if you have built yourself up to it, you can master it.

# GOOD SKIPPING HABITS AND PRACTICES

Setting a time and place for a regular skipping session and adhering to it.

Using a long rope, one that reaches from armpit to armpit when you stand on the center of the loop.

Finding your natural skipping speed and sticking to it while learning. Later, speeding up as required for various steps.

Learning to relax while skipping, so that each landing is on ankles, knees, and hips that are slightly bent.

Coming down on the balls of the feet in a "soft" landing.

Holding head up with eyes to the front.

Keeping both elbows and hands fairly close to the body.

Making small circles with the hands while turning the rope.

Practicing a new step first without the rope.

Practicing a new step (after the step is learned) with the rope turned by one hand, alongside the body, to get the feel of the rhythm.

Persisting despite initial errors until the body responds to the mind's orders.

Jumping low—about an inch or so for easy steps.

Mastering one step at a time till its execution is almost automatic before you go on to the next exercise.

Sticking to the training schedule (two-footed hops and running skips) until your endurance is adequate for more.

Skipping to a clock with a sweep hand or to a metronome at the beginning.

Refusing to be panicked by foot-and-rope tangles.

Always warming up with several minutes of muscle-stretching and joint-flexing exercises.

Always warming down by walking or "jangling" around after a skipping workout.

Counting your pulse rate several times during each workout to make certain the work is not too difficult. (See chart, p. 95.)

# MISTAKES SKIPPERS MAKE

Wearing shoes with heels.
Skipping barefooted.
Skipping on hard surfaces.
Using a rope that is too short.
Jumping too fast while learning a new step.
Jumping with a tense, tight body.
Jumping with eyes on the ground.
Holding the elbows too far out from the hips.
Turning the arms out too much at the elbows.
Using more arm movement than is necessary.
When going through the loop, crossing the arms at the wrist.
Jumping too high on easy steps.
Jumping too low on double turns.
Jumping and landing flat-footed.
Trying to put new steps and rope turns together too soon.
Giving up after a discouraging start.

# 8

# The Paul Smith Endurance Program

A remarkable physical educator named Paul Smith works for the Shoreline School District of Seattle, Washington. He is Coordinator of Health, Physical Education, and Athletics, and at the age of fifty-two he is a skipping enthusiast. His excellent book, *Rope Skipping: Rhythms, Routines, Rhymes*, is designed to improve the fitness of young people and is used by innumerable boards of education.

In the Pacific Northwest, thousands of people have seen Smith-trained units of rope jumpers performing at conventions and on television. He has initiated skipping courses all over his state and taught countless parents, teachers, and office workers to double their fitness. Once-frazzled mothers tell him, "It makes me feel so much better." Enthusiastic fathers say, "I can do so much more now than I used to." But the quality that characterizes all who complete his course, he notices, is their vibrant enthusiasm.

The Paul Smith program is based on the principles of interval training and a gradually increasing overload. It prescribes a series of brief exercise bouts separated by periods of rest. The early bouts are remarkably easy. A beginner does only sixty seconds of skipping per day, in four bouts of fifteen seconds each. Gradually the load is increased. For example, by the time the skipper promotes himself to Smith's fourth level, he is skipping through six thirty-second bouts for a total of three minutes per day. At the eighth level, he is skipping comfortably through six two-minute bouts. When the skipper can skip for eighteen minutes (with the rope turning at half-time) in one continuous bout, he has achieved excellent fitness and is prepared for more vigorous activity. This comes by simply turning the rope at a faster pace—up to 170 turns per minute.

I once asked Paul Smith, "Can you do all these exercises that you recommend?"

"I've gone as high as forty-five minutes without stopping," he replied. "I could go an hour if I had to."

His fitness is proof of the incredible efficiency of skipping. At an age when most men have retreated to golf and bowling, Paul Smith skips all winter and jogs all summer, except during the rainy season when he skips again.

So where does the average beginner start?

The easiest and safest way I know is to use the Table of Target Pulse Rates, below, in conjunction with Paul Smith's Endurance Categories, on page 102.

Most Americans do not know that their hearts slow down a bit each year. Swedish scientists, after measuring the heart rates of many thousands of persons of all ages, have struck an average heart rate for every decade of adult life, and their figures are accepted by physiologists and physicians all over the world. In one's twenties, they say, a heart racing all-out will average 200 beats per minute. Forty years later (in one's sixties) the best it can do is about 160 beats per minute. Why this happens is unclear, but knowledge of the phenomenon gives us a formula for safe exercise. The Swedish figures are the basis of the following Table of Target Pulse Rates, which is designed to help anyone to select his own safest heart rate. Just follow the seven easy steps below.

TABLE OF TARGET PULSE RATES

| | | Fitness Status | | | |
|---|---|---|---|---|---|
| | | 65% | 75% | 85% OF MHRA | |
| Age | MHRA* | Sedentary | Active | Very Active | Red Zone† |
| 20–29 | 200 | 130 | 150 | 170 | 180+ |
| 30–39 | 190 | 123 | 142 | 161 | 171 |
| 40–49 | 180 | 117 | 135 | 153 | 162 |
| 50–59 | 170 | 110 | 127 | 144 | 153 |
| 60–69 | 160 | 104 | 120 | 136 | 144 |
| 70+ | 150 | 97 | 112 | 127 | 135 |

* MHRA—Maximum Heart Rate for Age.
† Red Zone—Red is for danger. Until you have skipped rope for several months, you should not allow your heart to beat at a rate higher than the figure for your age shown in the Red Zone. An exercise that calls for more than 85 percent of your MHRA is for persons who are totally fit.

1. Find your age in the pulse rate table and follow it to the column which describes your fitness status: sedentary, active, or very active. Read the figures at the junction of your age level and your fitness status. That figure is your target rate.
2. Refer to Smith's Endurance Categories (p. 102) and select a trial skipping session, basing your choice on your confidence that you can complete the specified number of innings.
3. Warm up slowly by running gently in place for one minute.
4. Perform the skipping session selected.
5. After the final inning, sit down and count your pulse

for fifteen seconds. Multiply the count by four to get your heart rate for one minute.

6. Compare your one-minute heart count with your target rate. Note the difference. Are you on target?

7. Decide if the skipping level you chose is too hard, too easy, or just right.

If your heart rate after skipping is considerably lower than your target rate, you might try a higher level.

If your heart rate after skipping is considerably above your target rate, you must go back to a lower (more easily tolerated) skipping level.

If your heart rate after skipping is within a few beats of your target rate, you're right where you should be.

Understand that these target rates are approximate figures derived from averages. They are not sacred. Bend them a bit, if you feel like it. But do *not* force your heart to work beyond the figure in the column called "red zone." That is working too close to your maximum, which might be dangerous.

To make certain the above is clear, take as an example a sedentary forty-five-year-old man and see how he performs. First he reads the target-rate chart and learns that his target is 117 beats per minute (age 40–49 and sedentary), meaning that any exercise that raises his pulse rate to that figure will produce a beneficial training effect.

Next he turns to Smith's Categories and makes a choice. Let's say he was once a high-school baseball star and remembers his days of glory. He sees that Level 3 calls for a total of only two minutes of skipping. Easy, he thinks. Following directions, he skips for thirty seconds and rests for fifteen seconds. He does this four times, and is gasping for breath and has a red face when he sits to count his pulse. His fifteen-second count is 35. Multiplied by four, that's 140 beats per minute.

Already his pounding heart has told him that he has bitten

off more than he should chew. A comparison of his 140 pulse rate with his target rate of 117 is the proof. A 140 rate is for an active thirty-year-old. So he decides that he should start at a lower level. Level 2 requires a fifteen-second inning repeated six times. After a rest, he tries it. This time his pulse count after skipping is 120 for one minute. Close enough. He decides to start there and work up.

"Once you have decided where to begin," Paul Smith advises, "place yourself on the sequential schedule. Each individual must learn to set his own pace once it is decided where he should start." If you are not skipping comfortably at the end of any week, with your pulse rate after skipping in the vicinity of your target rate, stay at the same level for another week. There's no hurry.

Skip five days each week, never less than three times. Turn the rope at a speed of 60 revolutions per minute or thereabouts.

In the beginning, hop with both feet until you are comfortably coordinated. Then change to the running-in-place style of stepping over the loop.

**A word of caution:** It is wise to break in your sedentary legs over a two-week period. Skip a few seconds and rest. Skip a few more turns and rest. Your ankles and knees receive the impact of your entire weight with every hop. Aging knees can become tender. So can ankles, toes, and heels. Give them time to toughen up.

## THAT OL' I'VE-GOT-IT FEELING

Skippers are often puzzled as to why the simple act of jumping a whirring rope makes them feel so good. It's a delicate feeling, and no scientist will ever measure it. But if you master the art, you will achieve much more than better health and an enviable figure. You will know a succession of triumphs over a series of steps and routines which will blend ultimately into a sensation of delight and *can-do-itiveness* that can last a lifetime.

## LIFE'S DARKEST MOMENT

Beginners always remember their former athletic achievements and attack any exercise bout as if they were taming lions. The result is an early collapse, a feeling of frustration and discouragement, and a return to TV watching and snacking. Don't let it happen to you. Be gentle with yourself. Set your goal. And persevere.

WARM UP—DON'T HOT UP

Take it easy in the beginning. The warm-up is meant to heat the muscles from inside the body. Gentle, relaxed repetitions do this best. Paul Smith recommends "gentling in" the legs and feet for a week before you begin serious skipping. You will be tempted to turn your warm-up into an exercise bout. Don't do it. If you've got a phonograph, play soft music, slow and sleepy. Pretend you're a butterfly, not a jitterbug.

REFER TO THE CHART

You have a maximum heart rate that is determined not by fitness but by age. Refer to the chart on page 95 and note your target rate. Your objective is to drive your heart up to that speed but no higher, give or take a few beats.

In the beginning stay well below your maximum rate. After you've trained for two or three months, raise your sights to the active and very active level.

Now you have the information that can change your life exactly as it is changing the lives of many others.

You know how to train.

You know how to train *safely*.

You know the rewards, from better looks to better health.

You also know the penalties of failing to act. If you get a 9 or 10 foot length of sash cord and begin a break-in program for your legs, you will soon discover such joy in this perfect, rhythmic exercise that you will follow either the Rodahl program or Paul Smith's Categories until you have become as hooked on skipping as the rest of us.

## IF YOU BECOME DISCOURAGED

It is inevitable that during any fitness program a person may become discouraged. Exercise is effort, which in itself is a violation of the pleasure principle to which most Americans seem to be dedicated. So a time will come, usually quite early, when you will say to yourself, "I can never do it." Actually, the more anxious you are to succeed, the greater will be your chagrin, even fury at yourself for your ineptness. I've heard grown men berating themselves like fishwives. One was a Phi Beta Kappa who had become a self-made millionaire. In the beginning he seemed to be all thumbs and left feet. The expletives he flung at himself could not have been matched by most longshoremen. But he persisted through the vital first two weeks and became a skipping enthusiast.

For a beginner, the challenge is to develop enough skill to continue skipping without getting tangled hopelessly in the rope. The first five sessions are critical, often filled with frustration and fury. Stick with it. Hang in there. It usually takes about five days, sometimes a bit longer.

To make a beginning, I recommend the hundred-second test (see page 61). This is a simple hop-and-bounce performed in ten-second spurts. Here is the formula. Hop-and-bounce for ten seconds, rest for ten seconds, hop-and-bounce again, rest again—until you have hopped-and-bounced through ten innings of exercise and rest, or a total of one hundred seconds of activity and a like amount of rest.

Try it and note what happens. Are you out of breath? Can you laugh and talk without gasping? If so, you are making a good start. If not, cut back on the number of bouts of exercise and try again.

A virtue of the hop-and-bounce routine is that its ten-second skipping session is so short that one is unlikely to get tangled up in the rope. If one does, the rest period comes so quickly that it offers a new chance for success in the next inning.

Short, repetitive bouts improve coordination, skills, and endurance. Presently you will be surprised to discover that you are skipping more and resting less.

Several learners have told me, "I don't like to take my pulse. Isn't there a simpler test?"

Yes, there is. It is the talk test.

In some of my lectures I have talked while running in place behind the lectern. Frankly, it is a stunt to show an audience that running is easy and that an average citizen of considerable seniority can do it with no strain. Ordinarily I can jog in place indefinitely without running out of breath. But if I have missed my four-times-a-week schedule because of travel—or laziness—I find that my breath is so short that my words become mangled and smothered.

You can develop your own talk test. As soon as you have learned to skip, do a sequence of continuous skips (at half-time) while talking to a friend. If you are alone, you can recite a poem or even sing a song. After a while you will notice the beginning of some difficulty in speaking. All at once it is no longer easy to articulate in your accustomed fashion. (Everyone is different, but when I started I discovered that I began to pant like a dog after about 50 skips.) Make a mental note of the number of skips or the amount of time it takes for your talking to become labored. That is your reference point.

After two more weeks of training, re-test yourself in the same way. If you have been faithful, improvement is inevitable. You will be able to talk and skip for a longer period of time. Eventually you will have to work at turning your rope with real zeal to reach the point where conversation is a chore.

The process of improvement, by the way, is one of life's most heartening experiences. First of all, it means that you have slowed the aging process. Second, it means that your cells are beginning to work toward their optimum capacity. Saying it another way, you may expect many changes for the better in the commonplace experiences of your life. Your memory will become better, particularly if you are into middle age. Your nerves will be more relaxed. You will sleep better. Your emotions will be more stable. Your fatigue will probably vanish and is certain to be diminished.

So when you become discouraged, persevere: the rewards are within your reach.

## PAUL SMITH'S ENDURANCE CATEGORIES FOR BEGINNERS*

### EXPLANATION

**Level No.** This is a scale on which you can measure your present capacity and future progress.

**Turns Per Min.** This tempo is about the same as the half-time speed suggested elsewhere. A few more turns per minute or a few less are permissible. Do what comes naturally.

**Length of Ex. Bout.** "Ex." stands for exercise.

**Repetitions of Ex. Bout.** This is the number of times an exercise bout is to be repeated each day.

**Frequency Per Week.** To become fitter, exercise five times per week. To stay fit, three times.

## THE PAUL SMITH ENDURANCE PROGRAM

**Note:** First time through the categories, turn rope at half-speed and use two-footed hop and bounce. Second time, same rope speed but use the running skip. Third time, shift into high (turn rope at 100-plus), and do the running skip.

| Level No. | Turns per minute | Length of Exercise Bout | Length of Rest Period | Repetitions of Exercise Bout | Frequency per Week | Total Time of Skipping Daily |
|---|---|---|---|---|---|---|
| 1 | 60 | 15 sec. | 15 sec. | 4 | 5 | 1.0 min. |
| 2 | 60 | 15 sec. | 15 sec. | 6 | 5 | 1.5 min. |
| 3 | 60 | 30 sec. | 15 sec. | 4 | 5 | 2 min. |
| 4 | 60 | 30 sec. | 15 sec. | 6 | 5 | 3 min. |
| 5 | 60 | 45 sec. | 15 sec. | 4 | 5 | 3.0 min. |
| 6 | 60 | 45 sec. | 15 sec. | 6 | 5 | 4.5 min. |
| 7 | 60 | 1.0 min. | 30 sec. | 6 | 5 | 6 min. |
| 8 | 60 | 1.5 min. | 30 sec. | 6 | 5 | 9 min. |
| 9 | 60 | 2.0 min. | 1 min. | 6 | 5 | 12.0 min. |
| 10 | 60 | 2.5 min. | 1 min. | 5 | 5 | 12.5 min. |
| 11 | 60 | 2.5 min. | 1 min. | 6 | 5 | 15 min. |
| 12 | 60 | 3.0 min. | 1 min. | 6 | 5 | 18 min. |
| 13 | 60 | 4 min. | 1 min. | 5 | 3–5 | 20 min. |
| 14 | 60 | 6 min. | 1 min. | 3 | 3–5 | 18 min. |
| 15 | 60 | 9 min. | 1 min. | 2 | 3–5 | 18 min. |
| 16 | 60 | 14 min. | 0 min. | 1 | 3–5 | 14 min. |
| 17 | 60 | 16 min. | 0 min. | 1 | 3–5 | 16 min. |
| 18 | 60 | 18 min. | 0 min. | 1 | 3–5 | 18 min. |

* Chart from Paul Smith's book *Rope Skipping: Rhythms, Routines, Rhymes*, copyright © 1969, Educational Activities, Inc., Freeport, New York.

# 9

# Simple Steps for Fancy Dans

Thus far, the exercise routines we have recommended have been designed mainly to increase the body's tolerance for vigorous, continuous activity. This is what we mean by *endurance*. Its by-products are energy and enthusiasm.

One danger persists, however, and that is boredom. Americans cannot stand boredom: fortunes are built combating it, as Scrabble and TV soap operas attest.

So we suggest an antidote to boredom while jumping rope. It is a program of simple but interesting steps. Over the years thousands of skippers have introduced innumerable leg, arm, and rope positions, combining them into all kinds of jumping routines. They have used up to three ropes at once, sometimes with pairs, trios, and even squads of skippers performing in unison.

The following steps are easily executed, provided you have reached a satisfactory level of endurance. If you can skip without gasping like a fish out of water, you are ready to master them. If they tire you, continue to build up your endurance with your regular program for another month.

As the fact that you are a skipper becomes known, your friends will ask for a demonstration. Your regular endurance steps (the pepper and running skip) are impressive, but adding a few "glitter" steps really makes skipping fun.

More than that, your fitness will be maintained in an interesting manner while you increase your lightness of foot.

Second, you will gain in self-confidence—and self-esteem.

Third, adding glitter to your exercise period will increase your personal enjoyment.

Fourth, you will become a more effective missionary for "the perfect exercise."

## ABOUT PREPARATIONS

Be certain that your rope is long enough—check it by standing on its middle and holding the handles or ends against your armpits. A rope that is too short makes some steps impossible. If your loop becomes wobbly as you turn it, you may do better to get a slightly heavier rope. Sash cord is inexpensive, so try various thicknesses and weights until one feels right. The process is much like picking the right tennis racket. You pick it up, heft it, noting whether its "feel" gives wholeness to your swing. The right rope makes the same kind of difference.

## ABOUT STEPS

You have already used two steps for conditioning: 1. the two-footed hop-and-bounce (which later became the hop-without-a-bounce), and 2. the running skip, in which the feet alternate in stepping over the rope.

Your glitter steps will use these same steps plus a few others which will be explained as we go along.

## ABOUT RHYTHMS

You have been skipping to two rhythms, half-time and regular time. Your "glitter" steps will be done in one or the other.

*The half-time rhythm* is a slow turning of the rope during which you use the two-footed hop-and-bounce. You hop to let the rope pass beneath your feet and do a rebound, or bounce, as it passes above your head. When it reaches your feet again, you hop over it again.

About 60 to 70 turns a minute.

*Regular rhythm* requires faster turning (sometimes called pepper) while the feet do either a two-footed hop (no rebound) or a running skip. Speed: in the neighborhood of 120 turns per minute.

## ABOUT LEARNING NEW STEPS

Always try a new step at the slower, half-time rhythm.

Do it without your rope at first. The object is to get the feel of the unfamiliar movement before trying to coordinate hand movements with leg movements. Let the wrists learn later when you are comfortable enough to execute each maneuver without having to think through a procedure.

# Advanced Work

## BASIC FOOT MOVEMENTS

The advanced steps which follow use both the two-footed hop and the running skip, with variations.

The purpose of these steps is to increase the body's motor skills by establishing new nerve pathways, thereby sharpening your reaction time and coordination and increasing your ability to meet emergencies.

The brain commands, the nervous system and muscles respond, and a new pattern of activity is created. Repeat that pattern enough times and it becomes a habit. Each repetition leaves an imprint on top of an earlier imprint. Enough imprints (the number varies with different individuals) and you get the "feel" of the movement you are performing. When you have the feel, the brain disconnects, for all practical purposes, and you perform without thinking, automatically and refreshingly.

Hundreds of steps have been devised by experts, based on such primary movements as toe touches, heel touches, crossed legs, crossed arms, leg flings, kicks, and running skips that move the skipper from place to place. All teachers use the same primary elements though sometimes giving them different names. Teaching the fluid movements of rope and body through the rigid medium of words and phrases is difficult. One of those who does it best is Prof. Frank B. Prentup,* whose skipping teams from the University of Colorado have been giving demonstrations around middle America for more than a decade.

A number of his steps are included in the selection that follows. They have stood the test of time and performance. You can start with any one you choose, but it will be easier if you begin with heel-and-toe skips and work gradually toward the more complicated steps at the end. Don't expect to learn a step the first time around. Sometimes it takes a week. Remember that you are blazing new pathways for nerve impulses. The impulses ordered by your brain are stumbling through unfamiliar valleys in your muscles, which are lifting unaccustomed weights of flesh and bone. So stick with it. Master a series of glitter steps, work them into a routine of your own, and you will have an added sense of self-confidence. Most im-

* Professor Prentup's book, written for use in schools and homes, is *Skipping the Rope for Fun and Fitness*. It is published by Pruett Press, Boulder, Colorado.

portant, you will enjoy uncommon fitness and vitality, superior skill in sports, and—if you are overweight—a figure that proves no skipper stays too fat for long.

## SIMPLE TOUCHES OF HEEL AND/OR TOE

Professor Prentup says, "The learning process will be much faster if the skips and the turnings of the rope are practiced independently of each other."

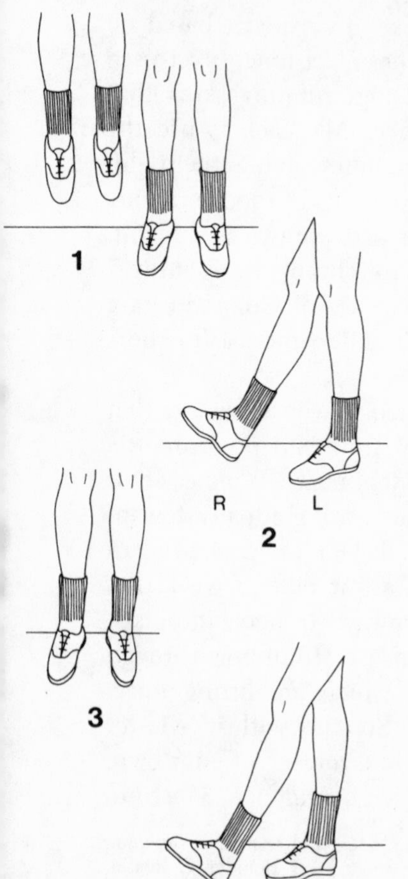


EXERCISE 1
(Tempo: 60–70 steps per minute)
RIGHT HEEL, LEFT HEEL

Action:
The legs are swung forward alternately to touch each heel in turn to the floor.

Directions:

1. Hop with both feet.

2. Swing the right leg forward and touch the floor with the right heel as you bounce on the left foot. (The heel is touched at the same time you bounce on the left foot.)

3. Hop on both feet.

4. Touch the left heel out in front as you do a right-foot bounce.

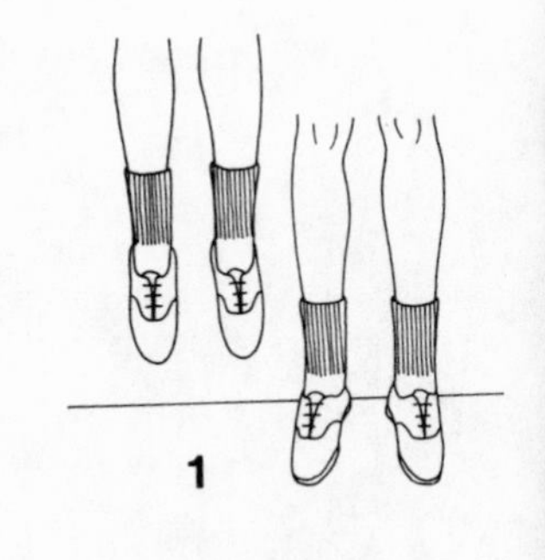


EXERCISE 2
(Tempo: 60–70 turns per minute)
RIGHT TOE, LEFT TOE

Action:
The feet are swung backward alternately and lifted up in back so the toe touches the floor.

Directions:

1. Hop on both feet.

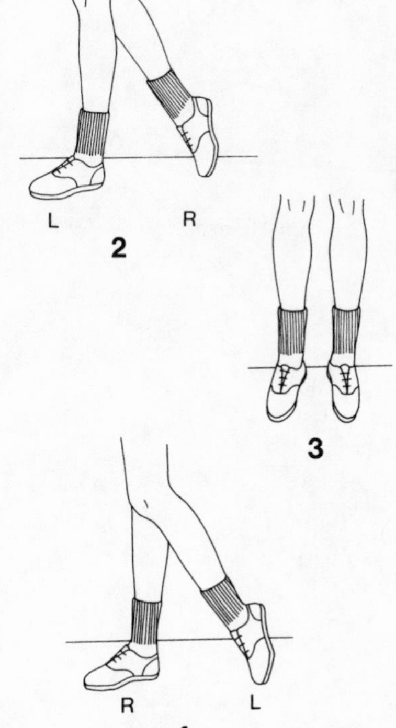


2. Bounce on the left foot and at the same time bring the right toe back to touch the floor.

3. Hop on both feet.

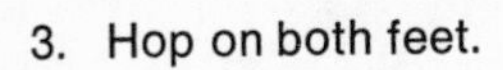

4. Bounce on the right foot and at the same time bring the left toe back to touch the floor.

5. Hop on both feet and continue at will.

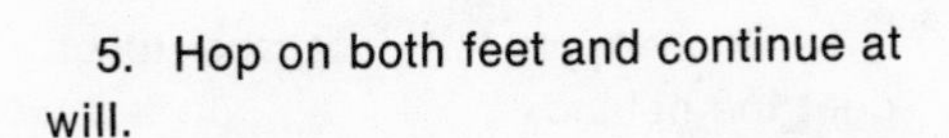

EXERCISE 3
(Tempo: 60–70 turns per minute)
HEEL AND TOE TOUCHES

Action:
As you skip, the right heel is touched in front and then the right toe in back, followed by the same step executed by the left heel and toe, all touches being done as in Exercises 1 and 2.

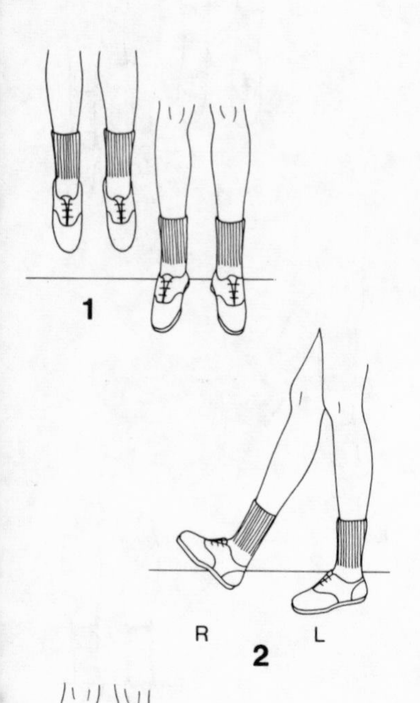


Directions:

1. Hop on both feet.

2. Bounce on left foot and touch the right heel in front.

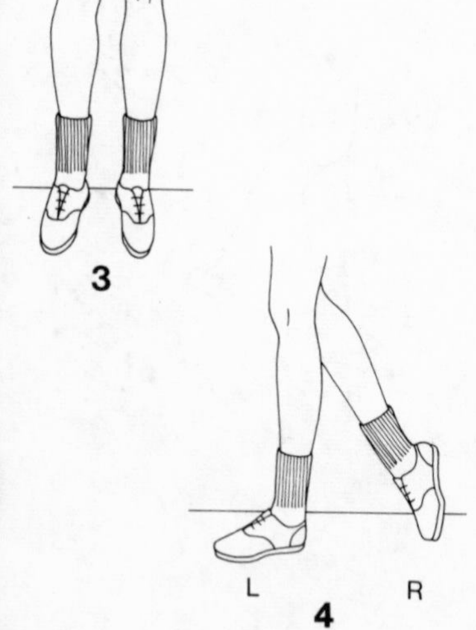


3. Hop on both feet.

4. Bounce on left foot and touch right toe behind.

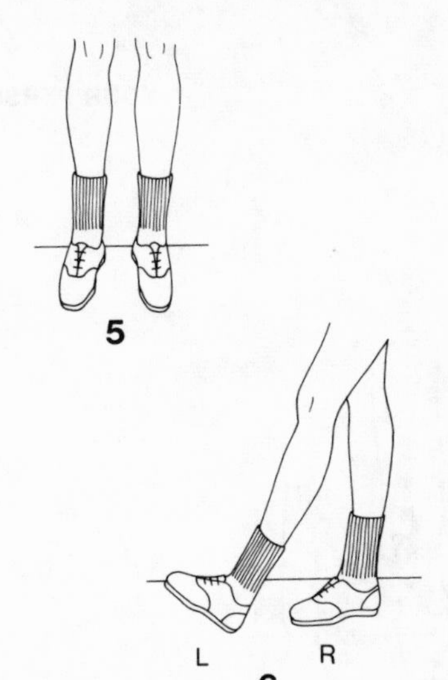


5. Hop on both feet.

6. Bounce on *right* foot and touch the *left* heel in front.

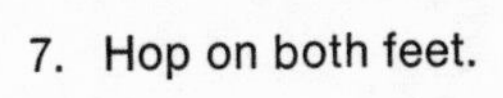

7. Hop on both feet.

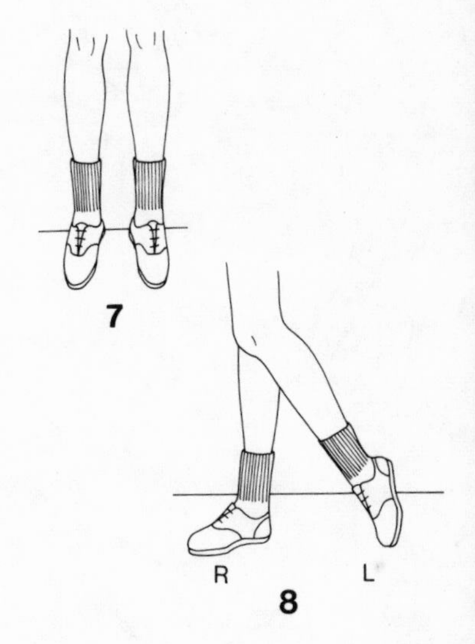


8. Bounce on right foot again and touch the left toe behind.

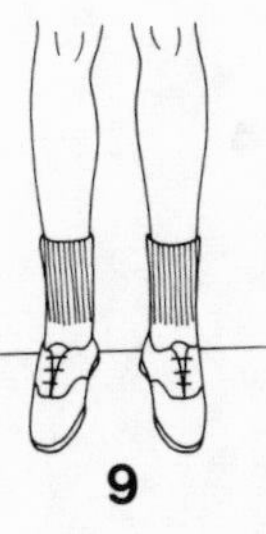


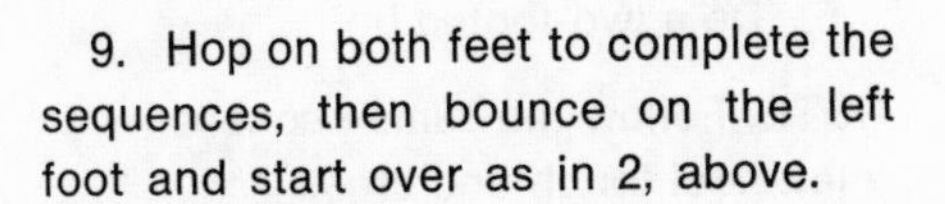

9. Hop on both feet to complete the sequences, then bounce on the left foot and start over as in 2, above.

EXERCISE 4
(Tempo: 60–70 turns per minute)
TOUCH YOUR TOE AND
CROSS YOUR FEET

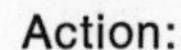

Action:
After a right-heel touch in front, the right foot is crossed in front of the left ankle, returned for a right-heel touch in front, and a two-footed hop ends the step.

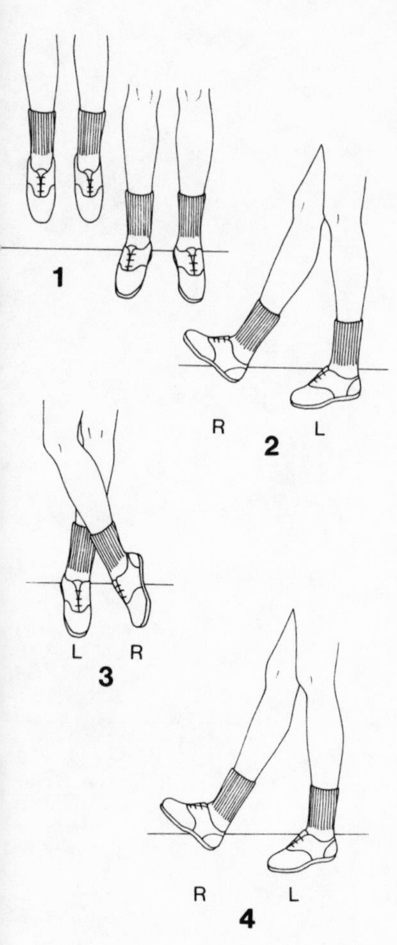


Directions:

1. Hop on both feet.

2. Do a left-foot hop and touch the right heel in front.

3. Do another left-foot hop, cross the right foot to the left in front of the bouncing foot and touch the toe to the floor.

4. Do another left-foot hop and touch the right heel in front as in 2, above.

5. Do a two-footed hop.

NOTE: Follow the same sequence with a left-heel touch and cross.

EXERCISE 5
(Tempo: 60–70 turns per minute)
HEEL, CROSS, HEEL, AND TOE

Action:
While you hop on one foot, the other foot performs a succession of touches, crosses, and bounces. It's very impressive.

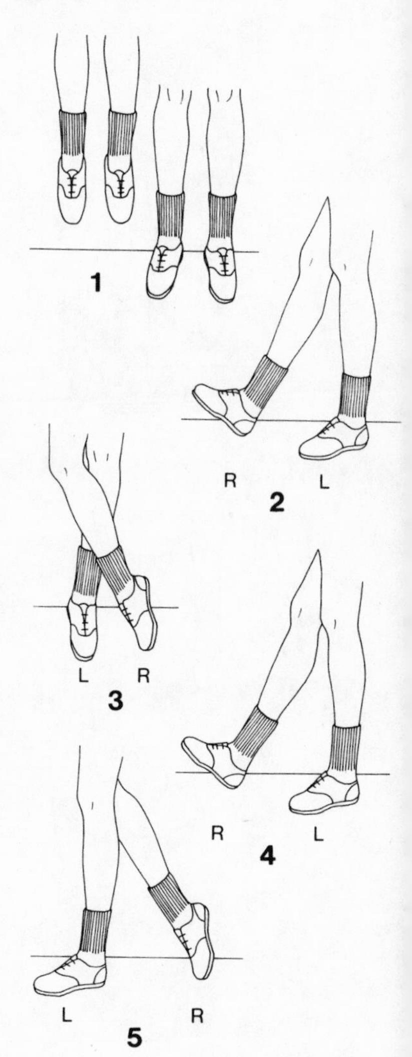


Directions:
1. Hop on both feet.

2. Do a left-foot hop, touching the right heel in front.

3. Do a left-foot hop, crossing the right foot in front of the left foot and touching the right toe to the floor.

4. Do a left-foot hop while uncrossing the right foot and touching the right heel in front.

5. Do a left-foot hop and touch the right toe in back.

6. Repeat, crossing the left foot.

NOTE: To reverse the movement, do several regular hops and then hop on the right foot while doing touches.

# SIMPLE SPREADS AND SPLITS

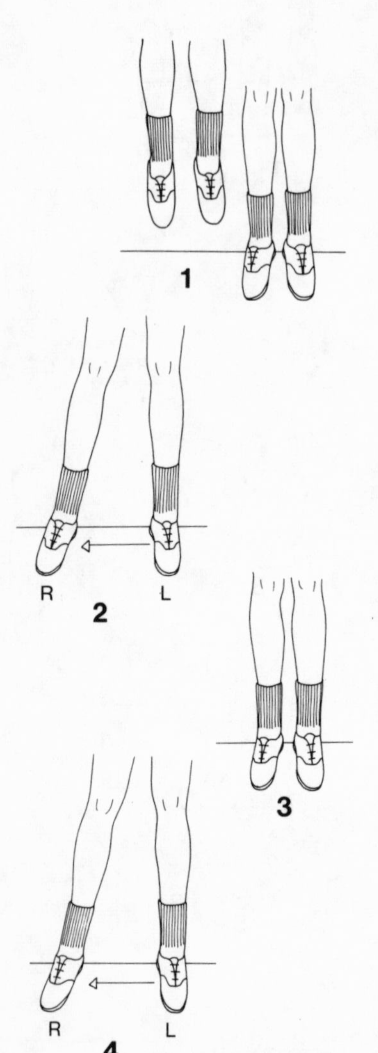


EXERCISE 6
(Tempo: 60–70 turns per minute)
THE SIDEWARD SPREAD

Action:
One leg, after a basic hop, moves out to the side to touch the floor lightly and repeatedly.

Directions:

1. Hop on both feet.

2. Bounce on the left foot and simultaneously extend the right leg sideward, touching the foot to the floor about 12 inches away from the jumping foot.

3. Bring your feet together and hop (a two-footed hop).

4. Continue at will.

NOTE: Learn to do the reverse action by hopping on the right foot and extending the left.

EXERCISE 7
(Tempo: 60–70 turns per minute)
THE DOUBLE-TROUBLE
ALTERNATE SPREAD

Action:
The legs alternate in spreading to the right and to the left.

Directions:

1. Hop on both feet.

2. Bounce on the left foot and spread the right leg to the right.

3. Two-footed hop.

4. Bounce onto the right foot and spread the left leg to the left.

5. Two-footed hop and reverse, and continue at will.

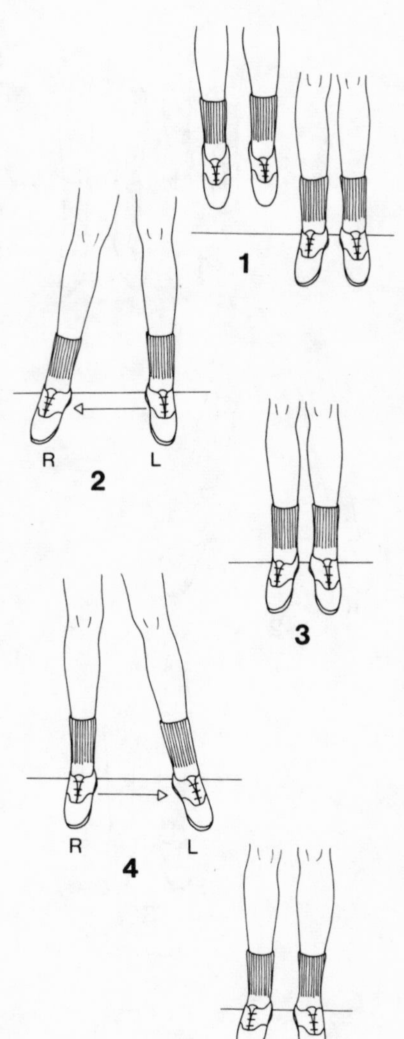

EXERCISE 8
(Tempo: 60–70 turns per minute)
STRADDLE AND SPLIT

Action:
The legs spread to both sides at the same time, while hops are taken with feet extended and centered alternately.

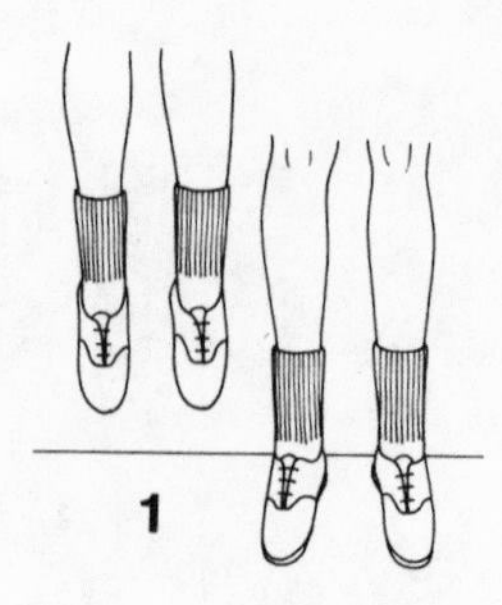


Directions:

1. Hop on both feet.

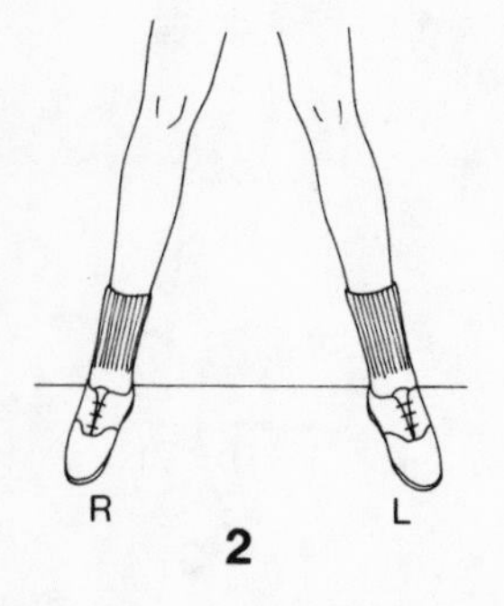


2. Spread both legs out to the sides in a straddle step, landing with the weight divided equally between the feet.

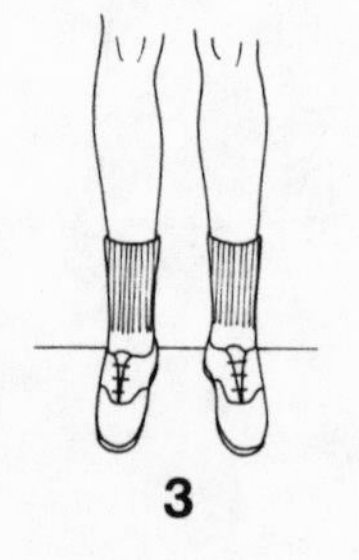


3. Bounce back to the starting position and do a two-footed hop.

4. Repeat at will.

EXERCISE 9
(Tempo: 60–70 turns per minute)
STRADDLE AND CROSS

Action:
The legs straddle, then cross, first with the left in front, and then with the right in front.

Directions:

1. Hop on both feet.

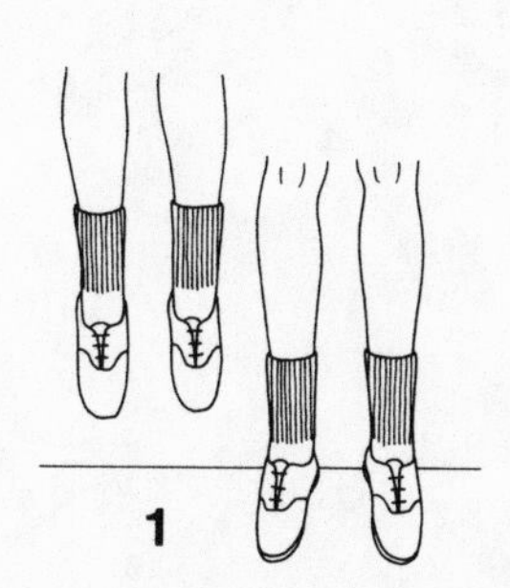


2. Spread both legs sidewards and come down in a straddle step.

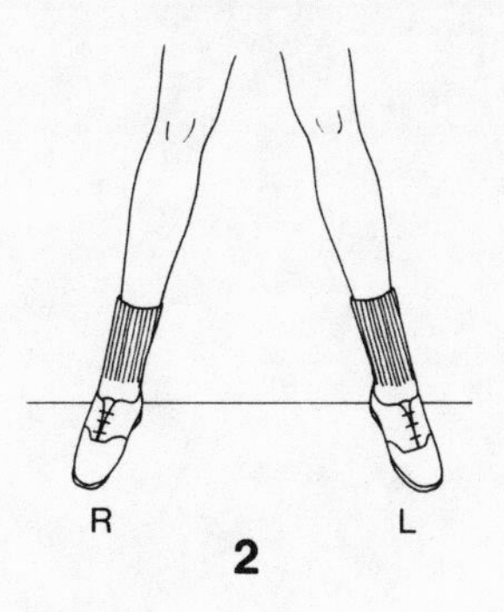


3. Jump and cross the legs, the left leg in front, landing with weight equally distributed.

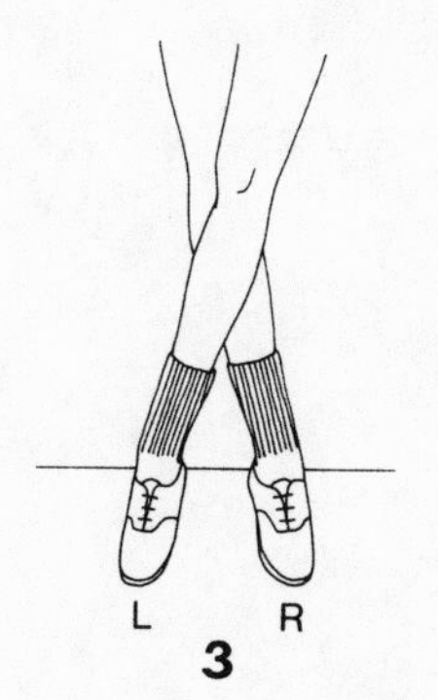


*(Exercise continued next page.)*

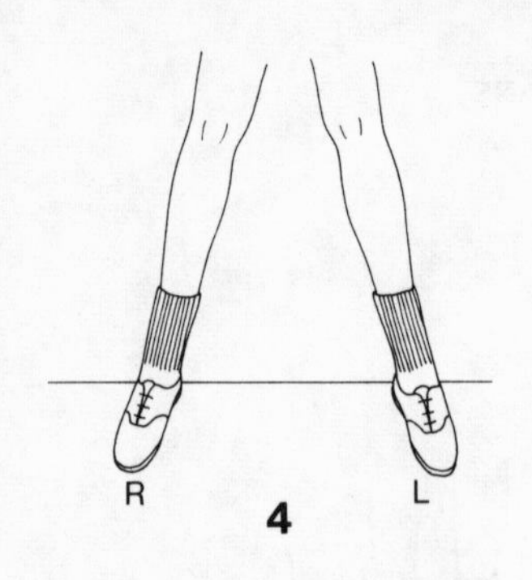


4. Jump and uncross the legs and land in straddle position.

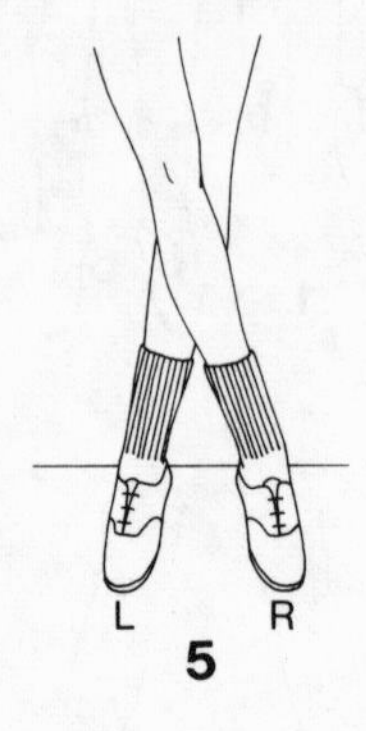


5. Jump and cross the legs, the right leg in front.

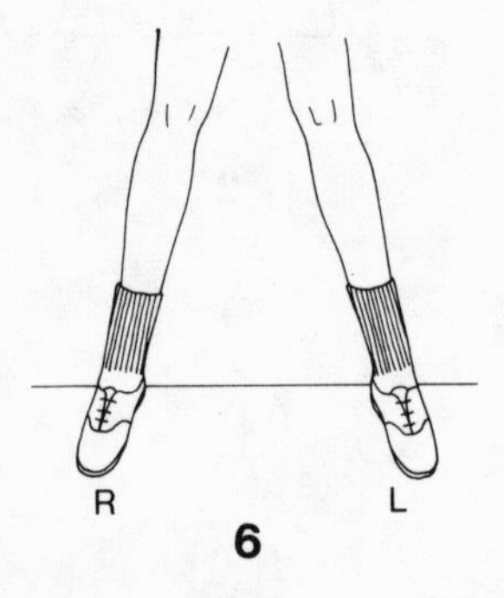


6. Jump and uncross the legs, landing in straddle position.

7. Continue at will.

# GIANT STEPS

EXERCISE 10
(Tempo: 100-plus turns per minute,
or, for an easier version, 60–70)
THE GIANT SCISSORS

Action:
This step is an exaggerated scissors step done in place. The legs reverse with each jump.

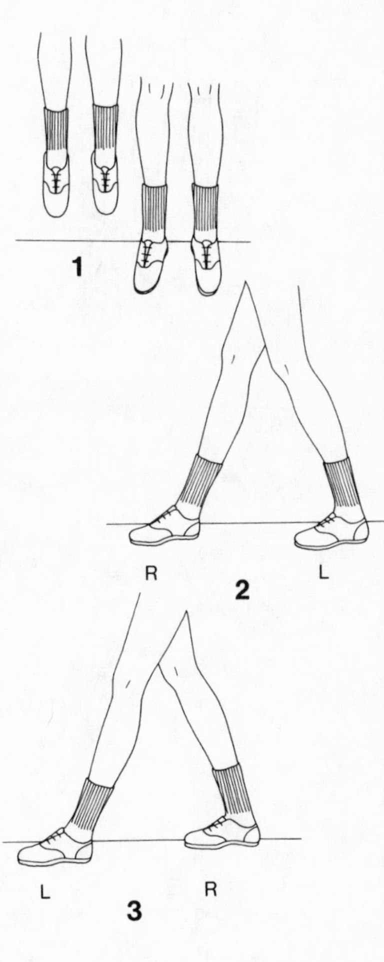


Directions:

1. Hop on both feet.

2. In midair, bring the right foot forward and the left foot backward, separating the feet as widely as is comfortable. Land in that position.

3. Jump off your separated feet and change legs.

4. Continue at will, scissoring legs with each hop.

NOTE: Slow time is somewhat easier for a beginner. When the rope moves at 60–70 turns per minute, the sequence becomes:

1. Two-footed hop.
2. Scissors.
3. Two-footed hop.
4. Scissors.
5. Two-footed hop, etc.

EXERCISE 11
(Tempo: standard speed of 100–110 turns per minute*)
THE GIANT ROCKER

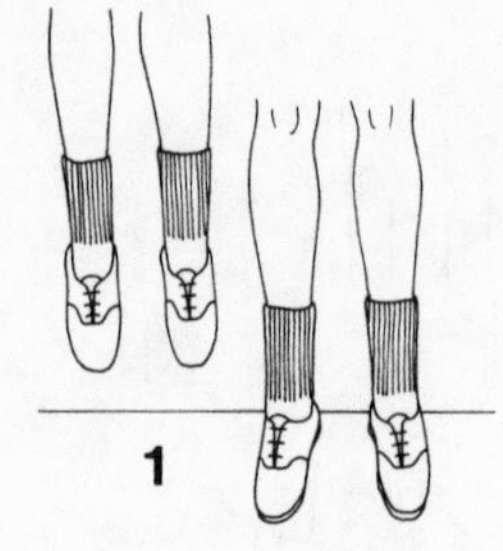


Action:
As the rope revolves, rock forward and backward, imitating the movement of a rocking chair or a rocking horse. This is a whole-body movement.

Directions:
1. Bounce until ready.

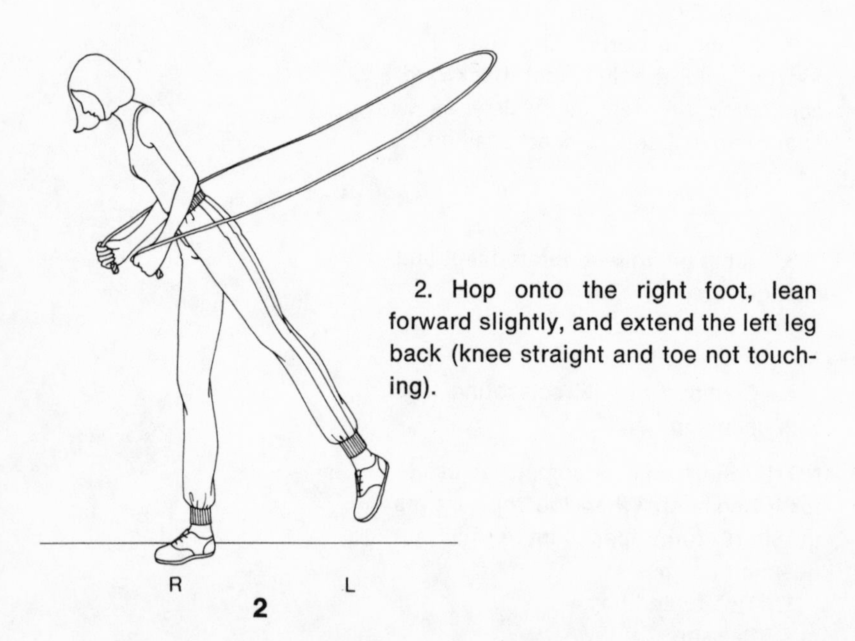


2. Hop onto the right foot, lean forward slightly, and extend the left leg back (knee straight and toe not touching).

* If you'd rather do this at half-time (60–70 turns per minute), the sequence becomes: 1. Two-footed hop; 2. Left-foot hop as right leg swings out; 3. Two-footed hop; 4. Right-foot hop as left leg swings out; 5. Two-footed hop; 6. Left-foot hop as right leg swings out, and continue alternating.

3. Hop onto the left foot and extend the right leg forward (knee straight and foot not touching). Lean back.

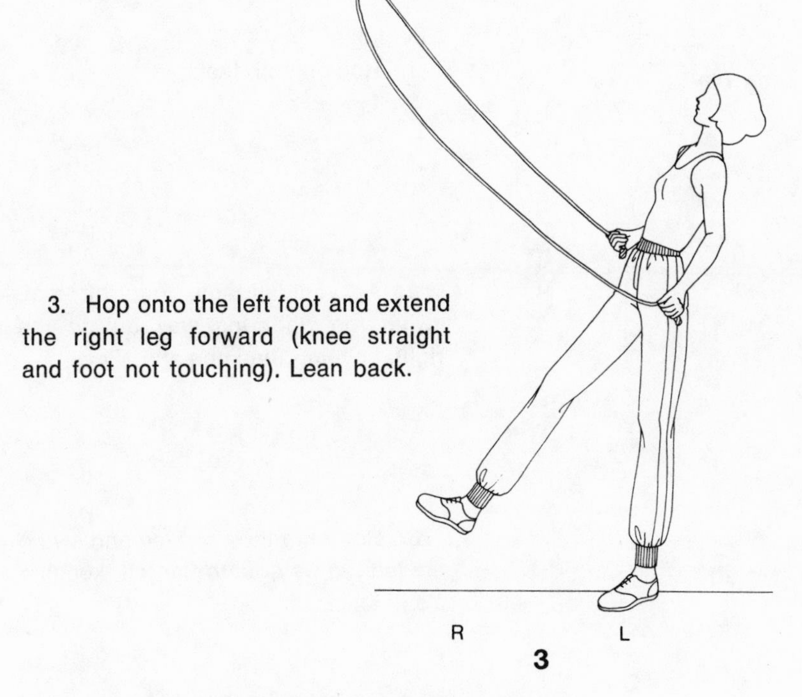


3

4. Hop onto the right foot and repeat 2, above.

NOTE: Your base of support is approximately the same spot for both right and left feet. The motion is exaggerated rocking.

*If you'd rather do this at half-time (60–70 turns per minute) the sequence becomes: 1. Two-footed hop; 2. Left-foot hop as right leg swings out; 3. Two-footed hop; 4. Right-foot hop as left leg swings out; 5. Two-footed hop; 6. Left-foot hop as right leg swings out, and continue alternating.

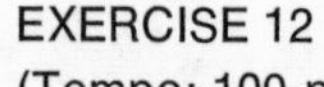

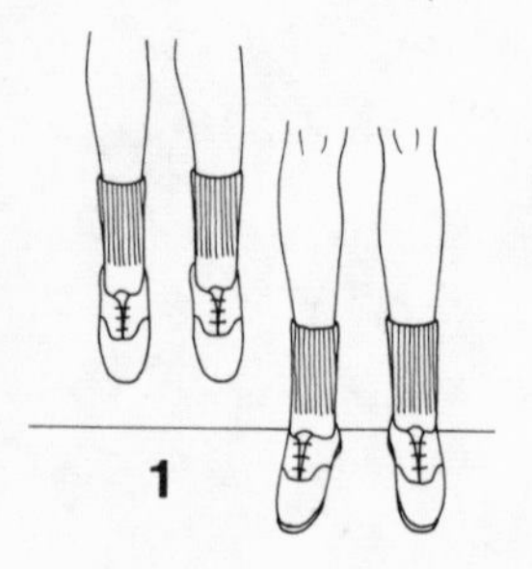


EXERCISE 12
(Tempo: 100-plus turns per minute,
or 60–70 for an easier version*)
THE GIANT PENDULUM

Action:
The legs swing from side to side beneath the erect body, simulating the action of a swinging pendulum.

Directions:

1. Hop on both feet.

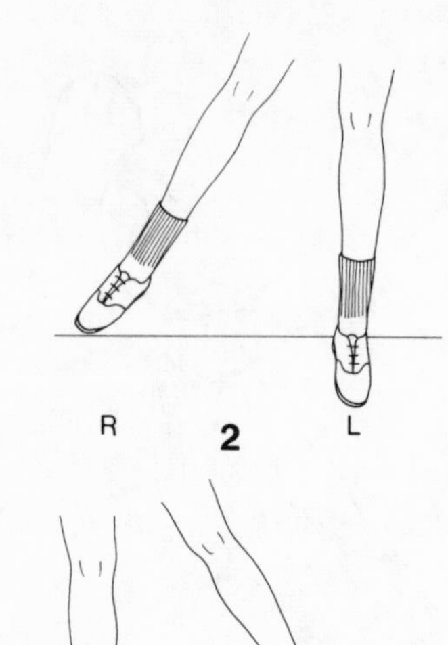


2. As you land on your left foot, swing the right leg way out to the right, keeping the knee stiff.

3. Hop onto the right leg and swing the left leg way out to the left, keeping a stiff knee.

R 3 L

NOTE: Your base of support is beneath the center of your body. One foot steps right into the footprint left by the other foot. As your legs swing out and back, lean your body to accentuate the impression of a giant pendulum.

* When the rope is turned at half-time (60–70 turns per minute) the sequence becomes: 1. Two-footed hop; 2. Left-foot hop as right leg swings out; 3. Two-footed hop; 4. Right-foot hop as left leg swings out; 5. Two-footed hop; 6. Left-foot hop as right leg swings out, and continue alternating.

EXERCISE 13
(Tempo: about 100 turns per minute)
THE GIANT DOUBLE FLING-LEG

This step has been done *without* a rope by comedians for years. Charlie Chaplin used it. Soupy Sales has done it on TV's "What's My Line." The bounce is much higher than usual, to give enough time for the legs to kick fore and aft from the knees in a kind of comic, midair split.

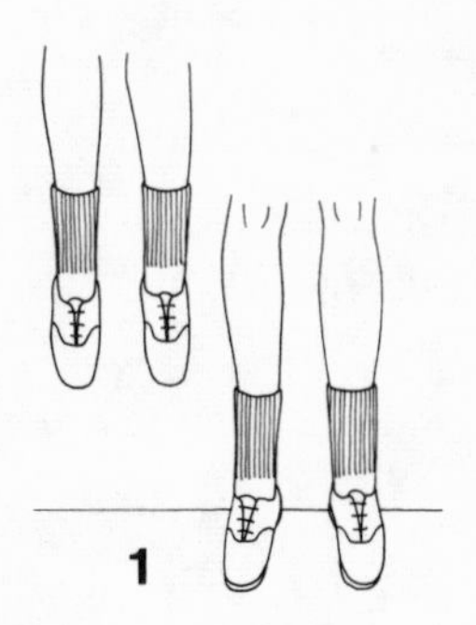


Directions:

1. Hop on both feet, higher than usual.

2. As you rise, keep the knees together and flip the right lower leg forward while flinging the left lower leg backward. Be sure the knees stay fairly close together.

2

R L

3. Descending, bring the feet together and jump high again, reversing the legs.

4. Continue at will.

# FIREWORKS

EXERCISE 14
(Tempo: suit yourself)
SIDEWINDERS, WINDMILLS, HELICOPTERS

Action:
These are rope movements performed while the skipper either runs quietly in place or does whatever comes naturally as he attends his rope. The intent is to spin the loop so its motion simulates the rotation of a windmill, a helicopter, etc.

Directions:

1. Bounce on two feet (the basic two-footed hop). Or jog easily in place.

2. Place both rope handles in one hand and spin the loop on a vertical plane beside the body. Hop or run in time to the rhythm. This is the *sidewinder.*

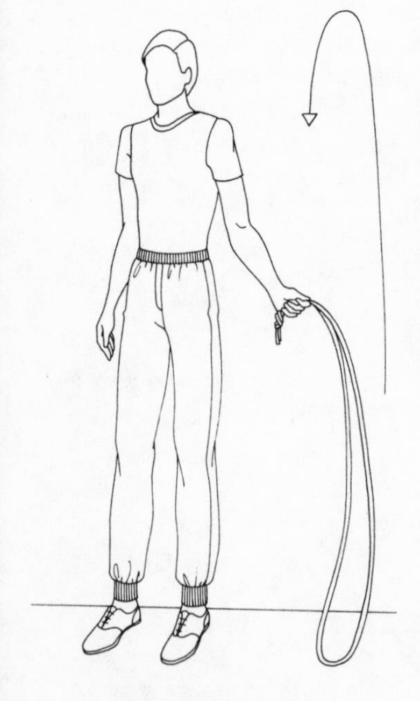

Sidewinder

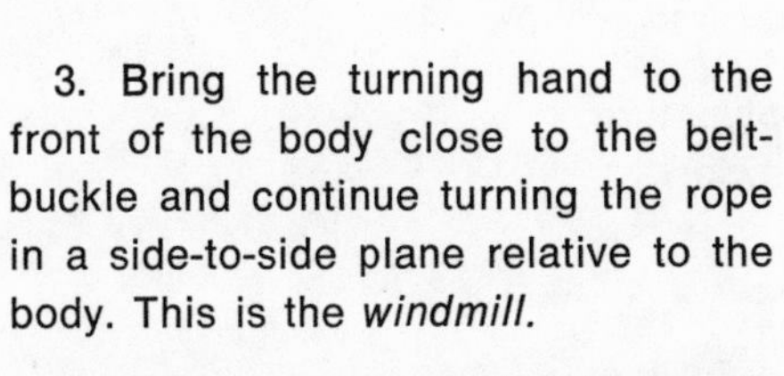

3. Bring the turning hand to the front of the body close to the belt-buckle and continue turning the rope in a side-to-side plane relative to the body. This is the *windmill.*

4. Lift your turning hand straight overhead and continue turning the rope so it makes a flat, horizontal circle. This is the *helicopter.*

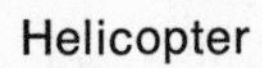

Helicopter

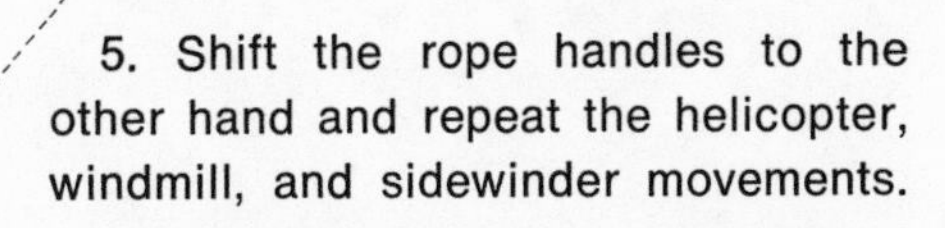

5. Shift the rope handles to the other hand and repeat the helicopter, windmill, and sidewinder movements.

6. Separate the handles and grasp one in each hand, keeping both hands at the same side for several sidewinder turns. Quickly bring one hand across the body to its standard position. This will open the loop so you can begin skipping again.

Windmill

EXERCISE 15
(Tempo: either 60 or 100-plus turns per minute; the latter is showier)
THROUGH THE LOOP

Action:
This is a stunt boxers use in their skipping demonstrations. While skipping normally, you cross both arms in front of your body and leap through the reversed loop.

Directions:

1. Bounce on both feet, till ready.

2. As the rope begins to descend before the body, cross both arms at the elbows and use the wrists vigorously to keep the reversed loop turning.

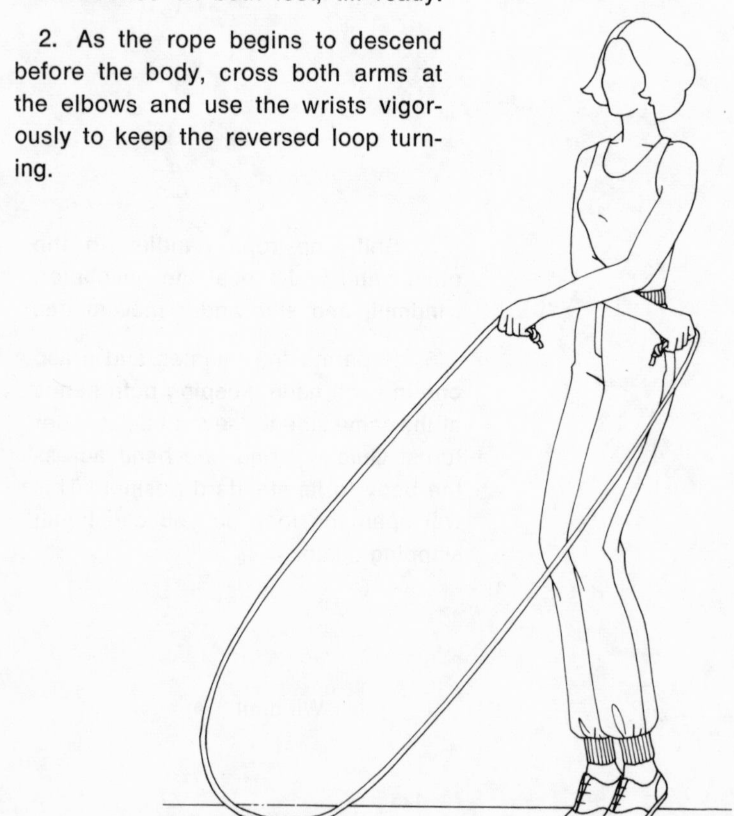

3. Hop through the loop.

4. As the rope continues on its next revolution, uncross the arms, whip the wrists through their regular turns, and skip as usual.

NOTE: Get the feel of this exercise and you can cross the arms at every other hop and continue skipping ad infinitum.

EXERCISE 16

(Tempo: suit yourself)

FLIP THE ROPE AND CATCH

Action:

Another glitter stunt, this one involves no actual jumping although the legs continue to hop and rebound gently. The skipper tosses the rope into the air so it makes a complete revolution. Catching the handles, he either resumes regulation skipping or concludes his demonstration.

Directions:

1. Bounce on both feet.

2. As the loop of the rope rises, thrust both hands forward and abruptly upward, releasing the handles, so the rope's ends rise almost straight up and the entire loop makes a midair turn.

3. Watch the handles as they finish their somersault. As they do so, grab them and bring the hands swiftly back to normal starting position.

NOTE: This takes practice. If you have seen tennis players tossing a racket in the air and catching it by the handle after a single revolution, that's the idea. If your rope handles are heavy, beware of being cracked on the head.

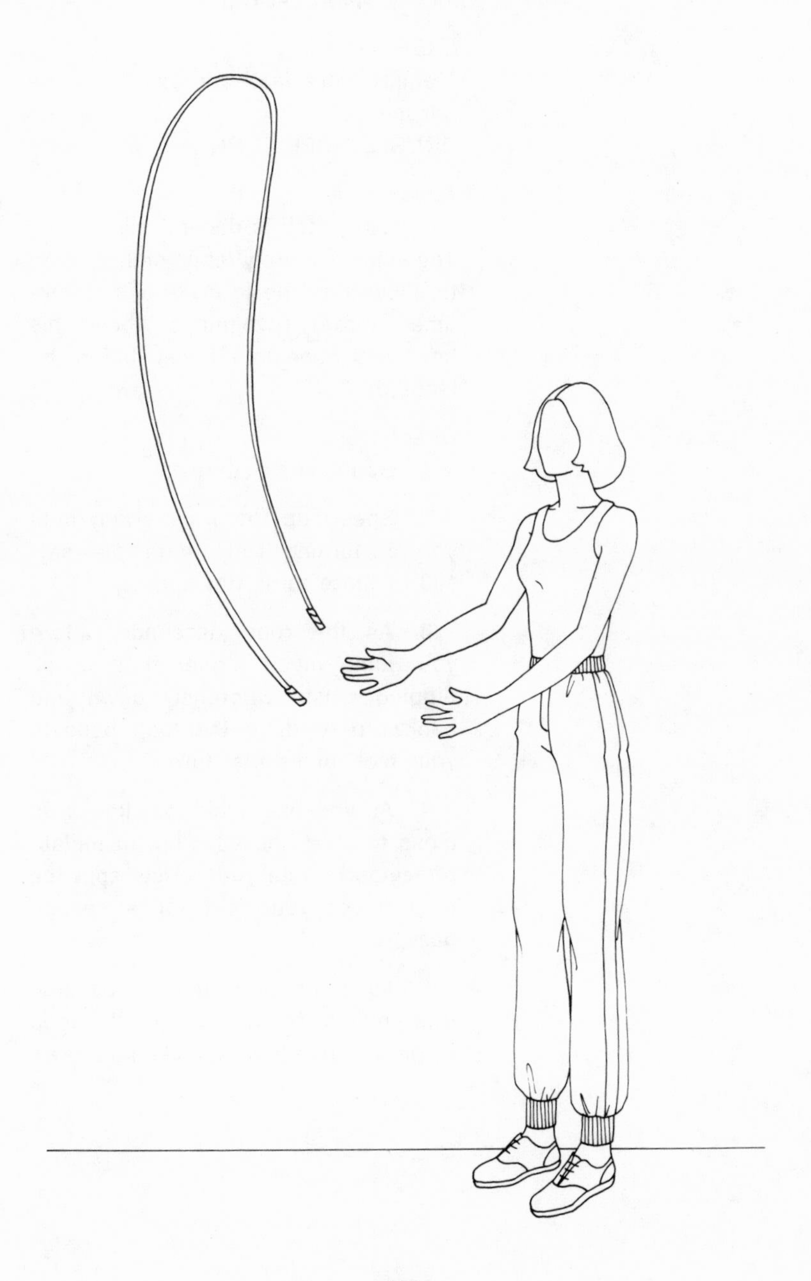

EXERCISE 17
(Tempo: very fast—approx. 140 turns per minute)
DOUBLE ROPE TURN

Action:
This flashy step is deceptively simple. The skipper merely leaps high enough to allow the rope to make two (sometimes three) revolutions above his head and beneath his feet—before he lands.

Directions:

1. Bounce on both feet.

2. Speed up the rope swing until you are turning it at a high rate—say, 140 or more turns per minute.

3. As the rope descends before you, jump much higher than usual, flipping wrists vigorously down and backward to drive the loop beneath your feet for its first turn.

4. As you rise, tuck your knees up close to your chest (you're in midair, remember) while your wrists spin the loop under your feet for a second pass.

5. Land in a crouching position (thus gaining more time for the loop to pass beneath your tucked-up feet).

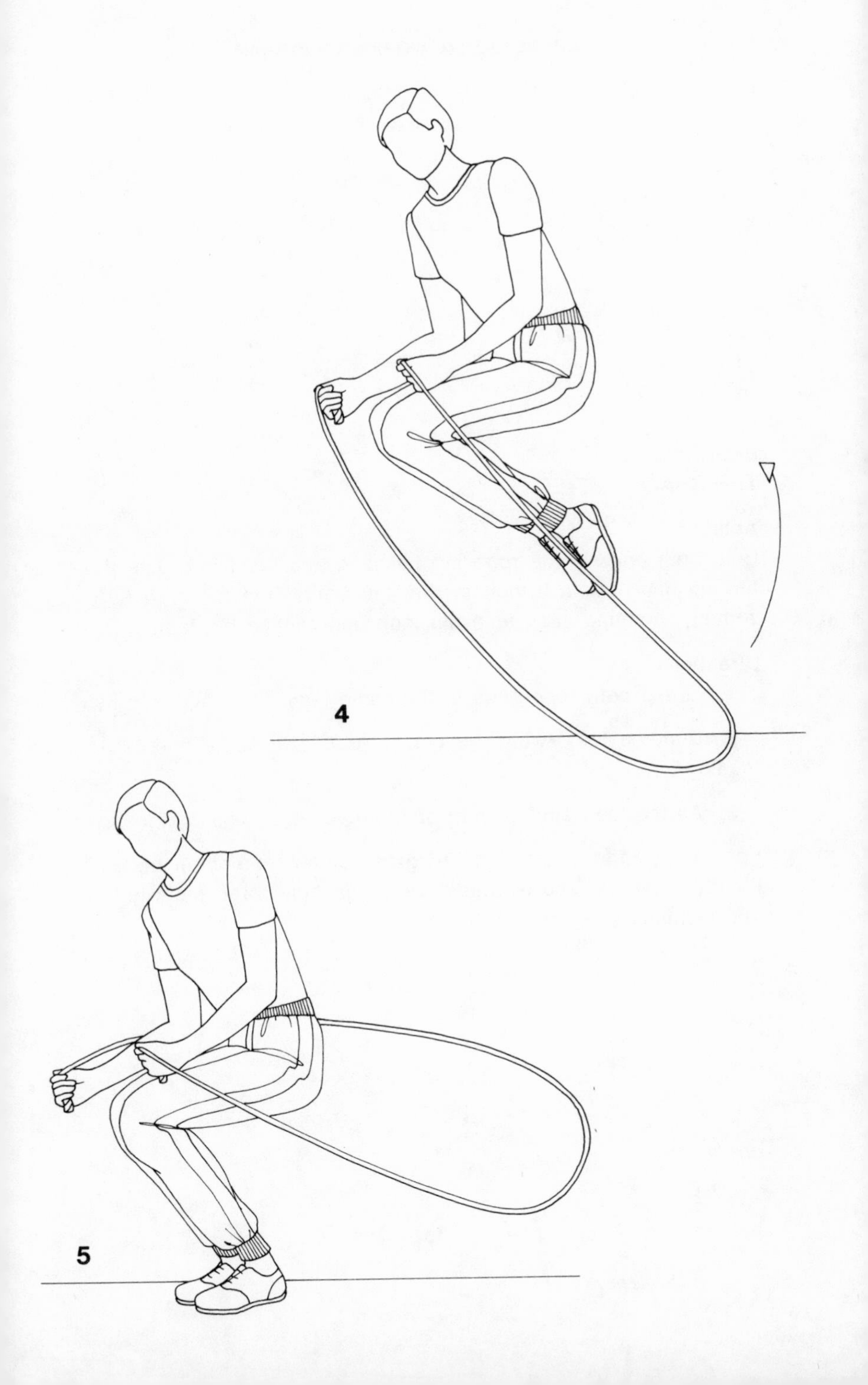
4
5

EXERCISE 18
THE GRASS CUTTER

Action:
Hold both ends of the rope in one hand and bend low, with the turning hand about 6 inches from the floor. Spin the rope horizontally, jumping each time the loop approaches the feet.

Directions:

1. Grasp both rope ends in the same hand.

2. Bending low, swing the closed loop in a circle parallel to the floor.

3. As the loop circles, step or hop over it.

For variety, after mastering the grass cutter, straighten up and lift the spinning loop overhead as in the helicopter, sidewinder, and windmill exercise.

## AND THIS IS ONLY THE BEGINNING....

Literally, there is no end to the number of steps, plain and fancy, that can be improvised by a well-conditioned skipper.

Rope skippers in Europe demonstrate routines in which the arms are extended straight out (like a scarecrow) while the wrists turn the rope (a much longer one than we use) through majestic whirls.

West Coast skippers have steps in which the rope is turned by one hand held above the head and the other below the hips. This takes extra rope, nimbleness, and concentration.

Another variation allows the rope to coil about the body, trussing it up except for the protruding hands, and then unwrapping the package swiftly without missing a beat.

Most old hands can skip while turning the rope in either direction, backward or forward. A few become expert enough to start in one direction, then execute a pause with the rope hanging in midair, and finally reverse their turns to continue skipping.

All steps in this book have started with the rope *behind* the heels, with the skipper turning it up and over his head, and stepping over it as it falls before him. Just for kicks, try turning it in the other direction, so that it starts *before* the feet, whirls away and up and over behind, and then you hop over it. Try it. It's a whole new ball game.

Part Three

# JUMPING ROPE—SPECIAL BENEFITS

# 10

# Use Your Jump Rope to Lose Weight Faster

If you are a member of the Great Majority who month after month troop into health clubs, spas, milk farms, group-therapy sessions, and doctors' offices, you are among the army of the overweight.

An Alfred Politz survey reports that 26,000,000 of us are watching our weight with mingled fear and fascination. Another 10,000,000 are actually counting our calories. We flit from one kooky diet to another. Any name that offers hope will do. Zen, Macrobiotic, Mayo (no connection with the Mayo Clinic). Calories-Don't-Count diet, Egg-and-Wine diet, Whipped-Cream-and-Martini diet, the Hollywood diet, the Nibble Diet, the Nine-Hotdogs-a-Day diet, the Drinking Man's Diet . . . All, alas, in vain.

One survey has shown that less than .02 percent of our millions of dieters take off their extra weight and *keep* it off.

But persevere! The malevolent spell of your tattletale scale can be broken by following a few simple guidelines. Know the rules, follow them, and failure is inconceivable.

"Eat less and exercise more," advises Alexei Pokrovsky, director of the famous Institute of Nutrition of the National

Academy of Medical Science of the U.S.S.R., who has supervised the reducing programs of 50,000 Moscow citizens. An advocate of exercise in short bursts, he discovered that a diet which took off two pounds or less per week would more than double the weight loss when supplemented by exercise.

Almost any kind of exercise helps, he says. Walking, swimming, pushing a lawnmower, pulling weeds, climbing hills, mountains, even the stairways at home and office, each contributes mightily. A jogger himself, he admits that running in place at home is just as good. Running in place over a rope loop is even better. And jumping rope fits his prescription of exercise in short bursts.

## WHY ARE SOME OF US OVERWEIGHT?

If we are overweight, it is because we overeat. But few of us admit it. The human ego seeks a patsy, refusing to place the blame where it belongs. The *Medical Tribune,* a publication which speaks for and to thousands of physicians, reports that "most obese persons are certain that their weight gain is not caused by what they eat. They are convinced that a quirk of their metabolism is at fault." So what do they do? "They seek someone smart enough to identify the quirk." They go from doctor to doctor, from diet to diet, seeking easy answers.

Your doctor will tell you if glands are involved, but the odds are against it. A careful survey of four hundred children disclosed only two who suffered a glandular incompetence. Forget the Twiggies in your circle of friends, who can eat all they want and never gain a pound. Almost certainly, your problem is within yourself.

In some respects nutrition is a mystery, but its principles are as plain as day. All food is divided into three classes—fats, proteins, and carbohydrates—each of which performs unique services.

Fat puts the sizzle in your steak and gives the heavenly smell to roast duck—it makes meat taste better. Fat represents energy; per gram, it produces twice as many calories as do either protein or carbohydrate. Fat dissolves certain vitamins so they can enter the bloodstream and supply insulation for frayed nerve cells. It comes from butter, whole milk, oils of all kinds, and meat.

Nutritionists say that we are healthiest when our diet is less than 40 percent fat. The average American's diet is about 50 percent fat.

Protein is the bricks-and-mortar of your body. When you are growing, you build with it, lengthening bones and muscles, widening shoulders and deepening chests. When you become an adult, you use it to repair injuries and wear and tear. Protein fights infection. Though it supplies energy, it is not a very efficient source. It comes from bread and cereals, dried peas and beans, milk and dairy products, chicken and eggs, fish, and meats.

Carbohydrate is every overweight person's choice. Each living cell depends on a speck of carbohydrate in its nucleus. If you fail to eat all you should, tiny sugar mills in your flesh go to work and manufacture it. If you eat more than the body needs, your internal chemical factories convert the surplus into glycogen, which is stored in the liver as an energy reserve. If some surplus is still left over, that goes into fat cells, a fall-back stockpile of energy. Carbohydrate is your body's "high-octane" fuel. When the body calls for a great deal of energy, it burns carbohydrate first, then fat, and finally protein. In your diet, its source is bread and potatoes, corn and dried fruits, sugar, syrup, honey, preserves.

Two more items deserve mention: vitamins and minerals. Here we have a general agreement among experts but also some disagreement.

The agreement is this: If you eat a well-balanced diet which supplies the recommended daily average of 2,800 calories for

154-pound men and 2,000 calories for 128-pound women, from four food groups, you *should* get all the vitamins and minerals you need. These groups are:

1. Grains and cereals—*whole*-grain
2. Milk and dairy products
3. Meat, fish, poultry
4. Vegetables and fruits

The disagreement is on whether or not you should take a supplement to make up for nutritional deficiencies resulting from food processing, cooking, storage, etc. One nutritionist told me, "If you are on a diet, be sure to take a supplement."

"Why?"

"Because your daily intake is calculated from a diet of twenty-five hundred calories, more or less. If you're on a thousand-calorie-a-day-diet, you are eating less than half your normal intake of food and therefore getting about half of the vitamins and minerals provided by a standard diet. So you've got to make it up."

Too many faddists think that vitamins are food. They are not. They are *catalysts*. Mixed with food, they cause nutrients to go places and do things. I believe in them and take them.

## IS OVERWEIGHT ALL THAT DANGEROUS TO HEALTH?

The penalties of obesity are no mystery. "Fat is a slow cancer," Dr. Melvin Anchell wrote in his book *How I Lost 36,000 Pounds*.

Insurance companies report that there is an astonishing parallel between extra weight and premature death. Alton P. Morton, former chairman of the Actuaries Committee on Mortality, says that a man who is 20 percent overweight increases his chance of an early death by 20 percent. And if he is 40 percent over, the probability of early death jumps to more than 115 percent.

More frightening is the relationship of obesity to killer diseases, physical dry rot, psychological trauma, and physical discords. One doctor reports that his fat patients have three times as much kidney disease, twice as much apoplexy, three times as much diabetes. "And the fat man commits suicide more often and has more accidents than his thin brother," he adds.

Fatness is blamed for initiating heart problems. Dr. Anchell says, "For every normal-weight person who has a heart attack, there are *ten* overweight persons who have heart attacks."

Hypertension? An extra pound of fat is said to carry an extra three-quarters of a mile of blood vessels. The heart, required to fill them with blood, must work overtime. Inevitably, the blood pressure tends to rise. Dr. Frederick J. Stare, of Harvard University School of Public Health, says, "A fat man's chances of getting high blood pressure are three to four times greater than normal. For getting diabetes, four to five times... of incurring major surgery, two to four times greater."

A fat man's heart rate is usually about 10 beats per minute higher than normal. His breathing is faster by about three extra breaths per minute, which counts up to forty-three hundred extra breaths a day. A person gaining weight almost always has a rising level of cholesterol in his blood, which can lead to atherosclerosis.

Other organs seem to deteriorate in a fat person. Gallbladder disease is traditionally associated with obesity. The skin may become striated from excessive stretching. The back may ache. And a man's testicles may cease functioning.

An obese person is usually awkward. Says Ancel Keyes, of the University of Minnesota, "Fat people are clumsy because their fat gets in the way. Arms do not swing freely and legs must move in circles in walking because the thighs are too fat to pass each other naturally."

So the heart labors with every movement, and the victim of our "clean-up-your-plate" culture feels his self-hate deepening.

A mystery that bothered scientists for years was why fat people who ate less than normal individuals either stayed fat or got fatter. Physiologists attached pedometers to a group of overweights and to another group of people of normal weight and clocked their daily mileage.

The fat men walked 3.7 miles per day. The thin men walked an average of 6.0 miles per day.

The fat women walked only 2.0 miles per day, compared to 4.9 for their thin sisters.

Whatever you eat, you must use it up in some kind of activity or else get fatter. Extra fat is stored when more food is eaten than is used. Even though the overweights in the study were eating less than the others, their lack of activity left a surplus of food in their bloodstreams. Acting on its million-year pattern of human survival, the body promptly stored it.

Teenagers fall into the same trap. A decade ago, traditional wisdom held that most obese children were glandular mishaps. Harvard's Dr. Jean Mayer challenged that theory with an experimental flock of fat and lean mice. He found that his fat mice were about 100 times less active than his normal mice. His next step was to study children. Hiding a camera nearby, he photographed them during play. Fat children acted exactly like the fat mice, standing around idly while their normal playmates jumped and tumbled. Even in a volleyball game, they were motionless 80 percent of the time. In one twenty-minute exercise period, they got only four minutes of exercise.

If overweight becomes obvious, the fat person may use it as a psychological crutch. Ruth M. Leverton, of the University of Nebraska, asked people why they ate so much. The answers are revealing.

"I'm eating to put off something I don't want to do."

"Something bad happened to me and I'm eating to forget it."

"Something wonderful happened. I'm eating to celebrate."

"I'm discouraged. Eating makes me feel better."

"Everybody but me has fun, so I'm drowning my sorrow in a thick, chocolate malted milk."

As the years pass, muscles shrink slightly and lose their tone. Being less strong, a person does less gardening, walking, or sports. But not less eating. So a portion of his intake becomes surplus to his needs. The body turns it into fat, depositing it in storage depots all over the body and holding it in reserve for a famine that never comes. Saying it another way, you become trapped in a self-perpetuating cycle. Moving less, you become heavier. Becoming heavier, you move less. Moving less, you become heavier. Becoming heavier, you move less.

A formula to carry in your head has been invented by Dr. Richard C. Gubner, University of New York:

*Start with the figure 36. Measure your waistline. Add your waist size in inches to 36. That total is your Fat Index and is to be compared with your height in inches. Your Fat Index should be the same or less. For each inch that the total rises above your height, the doctor says, you are 2.5 percent above your ideal weight.*

I tried the formula recently on my wife.

She is five-feet-three—63 inches. Her waist measures 29 inches. Her weight is 125 pounds. I took the figure 36 and added it to her waist measurement of 29, getting a total of 65. That's her Fat Index. The formula says her Index should be the same or lower than her height, which is 63 inches. So she is over by two (65 over 63). The formula also says that each extra digit indicates a surplus of 2.5 percent. Her surplus is two digits, or 5 percent. Five percent of her 125 pounds is 6 pounds and a few ounces. Objective—to shed 6 pounds.

No general agreement exists as to what is merely overweight and what is obesity. Dr. Gubner has his own formula: *viz.*, if you are six digits, or 15 percent, above your Fat Index, you are obese.

Check the table showing the *average* weight of men and women (by age and height), and compare yourself with the average.

# WHO IS OVERWEIGHT?

*Table A*

AVERAGE WEIGHT OF AMERICANS*
(in pounds according to height and age range)

| Height | | Age range | | | | | | | |
|---|---|---|---|---|---|---|---|---|---|
| | | 15–16 | 17–19 | 20–24 | 25–29 | 30–39 | 40–49 | 50–59 | 60–69 |
| | | | | | MEN | | | | |
| Feet | Inches | | | | | | | | |
| 5 | 0 | 98 | 113 | 122 | 128 | 131 | 134 | 136 | 133 |
| 5 | 2 | 107 | 119 | 128 | 134 | 137 | 140 | 142 | 139 |
| 5 | 4 | 117 | 127 | 136 | 141 | 145 | 148 | 149 | 146 |
| 5 | 6 | 127 | 135 | 142 | 148 | 153 | 156 | 157 | 154 |
| 5 | 8 | 137 | 143 | 149 | 155 | 161 | 165 | 166 | 163 |
| 5 | 10 | 146 | 151 | 157 | 163 | 170 | 174 | 175 | 173 |
| 6 | 0 | 154 | 160 | 166 | 172 | 179 | 183 | 185 | 183 |
| 6 | 2 | 164 | 168 | 174 | 182 | 188 | 192 | 194 | 193 |
| 6 | 4 | | 176 | 181 | 190 | 199 | 203 | 205 | 204 |
| | | | | | WOMEN | | | | |
| 4 | 10 | 97 | 99 | 102 | 107 | 115 | 122 | 125 | 127 |
| 5 | 0 | 103 | 105 | 108 | 113 | 120 | 127 | 130 | 131 |
| 5 | 2 | 111 | 113 | 115 | 119 | 126 | 133 | 136 | 137 |
| 5 | 4 | 117 | 120 | 121 | 125 | 132 | 140 | 144 | 145 |
| 5 | 6 | 125 | 127 | 129 | 133 | 139 | 147 | 152 | 153 |
| 5 | 8 | 132 | 134 | 136 | 140 | 146 | 155 | 160 | 161 |
| 5 | 10 | | 142 | 144 | 148 | 154 | 164 | 169 | |
| 6 | 0 | | 152 | 154 | 158 | 164 | 174 | 180 | |

* From *Obesity and Health,* published by the United States Public Health Service. Adapted from table on average weights and heights, Build and Blood Pressure Study, 1959, Society of Actuaries, Chicago, 1959, vol. 1.

Are you overweight?

Then check the table showing desirable weights for men and women twenty-five and over (by height and body type) and compare your real weight with it. Now how do you feel?

*Table B*

DESIRABLE WEIGHTS FOR MEN AND WOMEN AGED 25 AND OVER*
(in pounds according to height and frame, in indoor clothing)

| Height | | Small Frame | Medium Frame | Large Frame |
|---|---|---|---|---|
| | | MEN | | |
| Feet | Inches | | | |
| 5 | 2 | 112–120 | 118–129 | 126–141 |
| 5 | 3 | 115–123 | 121–133 | 129–144 |
| 5 | 4 | 118–126 | 124–136 | 132–148 |
| 5 | 5 | 121–129 | 127–139 | 135–152 |
| 5 | 6 | 124–133 | 130–143 | 138–156 |
| 5 | 7 | 128–137 | 134–147 | 142–161 |
| 5 | 8 | 132–141 | 138–152 | 147–166 |
| 5 | 9 | 136–145 | 142–156 | 151–170 |
| 5 | 10 | 140–150 | 146–160 | 155–174 |
| 5 | 11 | 144–154 | 150–165 | 159–179 |
| 6 | 0 | 148–158 | 154–170 | 164–184 |
| 6 | 1 | 152–162 | 158–175 | 168–189 |
| 6 | 2 | 156–167 | 162–180 | 173–194 |
| 6 | 3 | 160–171 | 167–185 | 178–199 |
| 6 | 4 | 164–175 | 172–190 | 182–204 |
| | | WOMEN | | |
| 4 | 10 | 92– 98 | 96–107 | 104–119 |
| 4 | 11 | 94–101 | 98–110 | 106–122 |
| 5 | 0 | 96–104 | 101–113 | 109–125 |
| 5 | 1 | 99–107 | 104–116 | 112–128 |
| 5 | 2 | 102–110 | 107–119 | 115–131 |
| 5 | 3 | 105–113 | 110–122 | 118–134 |
| 5 | 4 | 108–116 | 113–126 | 121–138 |
| 5 | 5 | 111–119 | 116–130 | 125–142 |
| 5 | 6 | 114–123 | 120–135 | 129–146 |
| 5 | 7 | 118–127 | 124–139 | 133–150 |
| 5 | 8 | 122–131 | 128–143 | 137–154 |
| 5 | 9 | 126–135 | 132–147 | 141–158 |
| 5 | 10 | 130–140 | 136–151 | 145–163 |
| 5 | 11 | 134–144 | 140–155 | 149–168 |
| 6 | 0 | 138–148 | 144–159 | 153–173 |

* From *Obesity and Health,* published by the United States Public Health Service. Adapted from Metropolitan Life Insurance Co., New York. New weight standards for men and women from *Statistical Bulletin,* 40:3, Nov.–Dec., 1959.

## WHAT CAN YOU DO ABOUT CONTROLLING YOUR WEIGHT?

Physiologists have spent many man-hours studying how to escape the fat trap. In general, those who are food-oriented recommend a diet that reduces the intake of food. One regimen is the 1,000-calorie-per-day diet. Some physicians will also try to depress the appetite by administering anorexigenic drugs (causing a loss of appetite) such as desiccated thyroid, phenmetrazine, diethylpropion, and benzphetamine. Their side effects, however, are sometimes serious.

Physiologists who are exercise-oriented usually specify a training program designed to increase the daily expenditure of calories. They want no surplus left at the day's end. Indeed, they usually demand a deficit.

Neither school has been wholly successful. The burden is too heavy. Joyous epicures are not about to relinquish their joy. Dedicated loafers are not about to begin increasing their exercising. But if you want to change yourself, something has to give. Dr. Kaare Rodahl reminds us, "There are only two factors involved in reducing: more exercise and less calories."

The Public Health Service cautiously asserts that "the most successful reduction regimen will probably combine some degree of increased energy expenditure with some degree of caloric restriction." Exercise a little more and eat a little less. It makes sense. It agrees with the experience of therapists. It imposes a burden so light that almost anyone can carry it.

But you need two props:

1. A bathroom scale
2. A jump rope

These homely tools are commonplace, but they can provide as good a read-out of your internal environment as most

$10,000 laboratory instruments. And you can learn to use them as easily as you learned to ride a bike or drive a car.

But first, the procedure by which food is converted to chemicals required by the body should be understood.

The process begins in the mouth. Chewing changes food into bits of body stuff, complex beef and potato molecules breaking down into combinations that can be absorbed.

In the stomach, the food moves on toward the small intestine, urged by peristaltic action. The digestive process continues. Some foods get there in five minutes; solid food in the stomach may take up to five hours. Carbohydrates are good travelers; proteins dally a bit; and fats simply do not like to move. They sit in the stomach longest of all.

In the small intestine, the food encounters an assortment of digestive helpmates from the gallbladder and pancreas, plus secretions which pour from mysterious fountains in the intestinal walls. If the meeting is normal, chemical reactions begin, resulting presently in new substances that are capable of moving through the intestinal membrane and eventually into your bloodstream. Ideally, every droplet of fat is emulsified by vitamins and bile and made ready for use as energy. Surplus liquid flows on into the large intestine. So does the residue of undigested food. There it is propelled slowly toward the rectum and excreted.

Each bite of beef Stroganoff, each sip of malted milk or dry Martini, is measured in calories. People count and condemn calories without really knowing what they are. Technically a calorie is a unit measuring the amount of heat required to raise one gram of water one degree from 15 to 16 Centigrade.

Nutritionists and eaters use calories to measure the quantity of food one consumes. Physiologists and exercisers use calories to measure the amount of energy they expend in various kinds of work. Thus the calorie is a unit we can use for balancing our food intake with our exercise output. Balance between intake and outgo is the guts of our program of weight control.

One pound of flesh is equivalent to 3,500 calories. To gain one pound you must leave an unused surplus of 3,500 calories in your body. To lose a pound, you must burn off 3,500 calories *more than you eat.*

To lose weight, you must create a deficit.

The first step in an eat-less, work-more program is to strip down naked in your bedroom or bath and inspect yourself. If you like what you see, fine. If you are in doubt, try the yardstick test.

Lie down full-length on a rug. Lay one end of a yardstick over your mons pubis (the slight bulge beneath your abdomen, just above the junction of your thighs) and align its length over your abdomen so its other end rests on your chest. How does it look? Does it form a bridge over a relaxed and slightly hollowed abdomen? It should. Or do its ends teeter in midair, its middle elevated by a mountain of your too, too solid flesh? If the latter, you have work to do.

Another test is the pinch test. Even healthy people have a thin layer of fat, and the fact that it exists is normal. It causes trouble only when it thickens into pillows and spare tires. Fortunately you can pinch it up between thumb and forefinger and gauge its thickness.

Try the skin on the back of your hand. Pinch up a fold. Rub thumb and forefinger together and feel the fat layer beneath. There's not much fat there; your hands stay fit because they exercise so much.

Try it on your tricep (the rear portion of the upper arm). Here the fat layer in a normal person should be from ¼ to ½ inch thick. Since your pinch lifts up a fold, your thumb and forefinger will be separated by two thicknesses of fat and skin. The allowable maximum is 1 inch. Slightly less is better. If your pinch is more than an inch thick, you had better start counting calories and exercising more.

Finally, pick a spot on your abdomen near the belly button and pinch up a fold. This may be difficult. If your pinch measures less than one inch, you are in fine shape. If it measures more, you should pay special attention to the next paragraphs.

If you did not pass your test, then you need a program which will provide a daily *deficit* of calories. If you want to hold on to your present good looks, you need a program that will *balance* your caloric input and outgo. In either case, your closest friend is the scale in your bathroom. The best way to keep track of your weight is to weigh naked every morning before breakfast and enter the figure on a chart. You could keep it in your head, but writing down your weight reinforces your resolution. So make a chart like the one below, and tape it to your mirror. A 3″ × 5″ index card will do. Draw six vertical lines across it, making seven spaces, one for each day of the week.

At the top, write the words: WHAT GOES ON HERE?

This chart is to report exactly what is happening during one week in the real world of your life. For seven straight days, enter your weight. Note any changes from day to day. If there are none, your intake and output are stabilized. If you are

What Goes on Here?

| Su | M | T | W | Th | F | Sa |
|---|---|---|---|---|---|---|
| 157 | 157 | 156 | 156 | 156 | 155 | 154 |
| 155 | 154 | 154 | 153 | | | |

gaining, the trend will be up. If you are losing, happy thought, you'll be the first to know. If the record of one week does not tell you convincingly of what goes on, extend this dry run for another week.

What about a chart for the weeks or months of your program? It depends on your personal psychology. Some doctors do not allow their patients to weigh themselves, claiming that they get too discouraged. Others insist on it, citing benefits.

In Washington, D.C., Prof. Joe Lee Jessup, of George Washington University, steps confidently onto his scales each morning and enters his weight in a tattered weight diary. "It forces me to make a daily commitment," he says. "When I've lost some pounds, I stay down."

An obese oil executive in Oklahoma City became so fascinated with his daily weight changes that he made up a huge chart and hung it across one wall of his office. Daily losses were exhibited in king-size digits.

A California housewife steps on two scales, one for each foot. A bathroom scale ordinarily weighs only up to 250 pounds. Her starting weight was 312. She notes the weight on each scale, adds them together, and records her total.

Dr. Robert C. Atkins, of New York City, specializes in carbohydrate metabolism. He advises, "Weigh in every morning when you brush your teeth. Everything begins with awareness. Using the scale makes you more aware of your problem and that is the prelude to action."

Pick your objective! The ideal-weight table on page 145 can be your guide. What's a rule of thumb? The late Dr. Paul Dudley White asked his patients to try to regain the weight they enjoyed at age twenty-five.

Regardless of how much you want to lose, the important factor is the *rate of loss*. Some diets offer a quick loss of five or ten pounds in the first week. Beware: It is mostly water and not fat, and water always returns. Physiologists with experience in this field usually seek a loss of one or two pounds per week. Either is safe, so take your choice. Let's say you choose the slower pace.

You already know that a pound of fat is equivalent to 3,500 calories. To lose 3,500 calories in one week of seven days, you must run a calorie deficit of 500 calories each day (500 calories × 7 days = 3,500 calories).

And you must continue to do this for all the days between now and the day your goal is attained. It may be closer than you think!

Your goal of 500 calories per day can be achieved in any way you want, either by eating less or exercising more. When the two are combined, it is easier.

*Your Daily Weight-Control Program*

1. You eat less than your usual diet by 250 calories.
2. You exercise more than is your habit by 250 calories.

Total Loss per Day = 500 calories.
500 calories × seven days = 3,500 calories—one pound.

In eating less, you will obviously avoid pie à la mode, chocolate malts, and double Scotches. Bonnie Prudden, famous author, teacher, and lecturer on physical fitness, once showed me a Fright List that she asks her clients to hang on their walls. Some of its items were:

| | |
|---|---|
| Ice cream soda | 300 cal. |
| Hamburger/Cheeseburger | 400 |
| Peanut butter sandwich | 350 |
| Club sandwich | 450 |
| Whole milk, per glass | 225 |
| Mayonnaise—a dollop | 100 |
| French fries—1 cup | 200 |
| Hotdog and bun | 225 |
| Popcorn at the movies | 400 |
| Pie | 400 |

You will avoid such monstrosities at all costs. When you

weigh yourself and write down your weight, you make a commitment. But also think in specifics: "Today, I'll skip that extra pancake at breakfast and after-dinner dessert." Right there you are saving 250 calories.

Everyone who diets loves to talk about dieting. Psychologists say it hurts. Try to keep your diet a secret. Myths abound, and so do diet-centered controversies. Keep an open mind and don't go overboard for any fad. Eat balanced meals that come from the farm and barn: whole-grain breads, milk and milk products, fruits and vegetables, and meats of all kinds. Such meals automatically balance themselves. Make certain you are getting an abundance of protein and carbohydrate. Keep the level of fat down, but don't ever try to eliminate it.

Dr. Jean Mayer, of the School of Public Health of Harvard University, says, "A balanced diet, comprising no less than 14 percent protein, no more than 30 percent fat (with saturated fats cut down), and the rest carbohydrates (with sugar cut down to a low level) is still the best diet."

## WHAT DOES EXERCISE DO FOR WEIGHT REDUCTION?

What about exercise, and how does a jump rope help? The processes which sustain your life at its lowest ebb (sleeping) require an average of 75 to 80 calories per hour. Sitting up costs an extra 15 calories. Standing—140 per hour. Roller skating—350. Hill climbing—540. Every move you make burns off extra calories. In time, they add up. If your total "burn-off" is larger than your intake, you lose weight.

Ride your bike daily for an extra hour on level ground and you may lose from three-quarters to a pound of fat per week, according to your speed.

Swim daily for sixty minutes (but really swim) and you may lose two pounds per week.

Tennis consumes calories even faster than swimming.

It might help to think of yourself as an automobile with a tank full of *fat*. Rolling along at a moderate speed, you get a certain mileage. Put your foot on the accelerator and speed up, and you begin to burn more fat. The faster you go, the bigger the "burn," and gradually the fat tank empties. If your car were a human body, it would get slimmer. For the calorie "burn" of different kinds of exercise, see the chart on page 154. Select whatever exercises fit best into your way of life, and work them into your daily routine. Somebody has said that it is impossible to *find* time for exercise. You have to *make* time for it.

Of all weight-control exercises, to me, jumping rope is the best and among the most efficient.

With a jump rope you can reduce your overweight in brief sessions repeated a half-dozen times a day. I know of one woman who hangs her rope near her garden house and augments her chores with one minute of jumping before and after. Another parks her rope in the garage beside her car. Returning from a shopping trip, she enjoys a thirty-second session. A businessman turns his coffee break into a skipping break.

The burn-off from skipping is very high, over 720 calories per hour. But other activities need not be neglected. Any day can offer a variety of sports, games, and exercises: jump a little; climb stairs twice as often as usual; play golf or tennis or catch with the kids; swim or do push-ups.

Invent stunts. When you skip, make every fourth jump a high one, or see how deeply you can bend your knees. The best reducing regime is the one that uses the widest possible variety of energetic activities. By adding skipping to walking, with energy, you will shed pounds and turn fat to muscle.

The object is to eat a little less, exercise a little more, and not only will you lose weight, but those pounds and inches of flab will stay off for good.

ENERGY EXPENDITURE BY A 150 POUND PERSON IN VARIOUS ACTIVITIES*

| Activity | Gross Energy Cost-Cal per hr. |
|---|---|
| A. Rest and Light Activity | 80–200 |
| Lying down or sleeping | 80 |
| Sitting | 100 |
| Driving an automobile | 120 |
| Standing | 140 |
| Domestic work | 180 |
| B. Moderate Activity | 200–350 |
| Bicycling (5½ mph) | 210 |
| Walking (2½ mph) | 210 |
| Gardening | 220 |
| Canoeing (2½ mph) | 230 |
| Golf | 250 |
| Lawn mowing (power mower) | 250 |
| Bowling | 270 |
| Lawn mowing (hand mower) | 270 |
| Rowboating (2½ mph) | 300 |
| Swimming (¼ mph) | 300 |
| Walking (3¾ mph) | 300 |
| Badminton | 350 |
| Horseback riding (trotting) | 350 |
| Square dancing | 350 |
| Volleyball | 350 |
| C. Vigorous Activity | over 350 |
| Table tennis | 360 |
| Ice skating (10 mph) | 400 |
| Wood chopping or sawing | 400 |
| Tennis | 420 |
| Water skiing | 480 |
| Hill climbing (100 ft. per hr.) | 490 |
| Skiing (10 mph) | 600 |
| Squash and handball | 600 |
| Cycling (13 mph) | 660 |
| Running (5.7 mph) | 720 |
| Skipping rope (120–140 turns per min.) | 720† |
| Scull rowing (race) | 840 |
| Running (10 mph) | 900 |

* The standards represent a compromise between those proposed by the British Medical Association (1950), Christensen (1953) and Wells, Balke, and Van Fossan (1956). Where available, actual measured values have been used; for other values a "best guess" was made.

† Energy cost of skipping inserted by author for easy comparison.

# 11

# Use Your Jump Rope to Protect Your Heart

About 150,000 Americans will die of coronary disease *this week*—and for every foreseeable week in the future. Citizens of more than a dozen other countries will outlive us by years, and those of Sweden will live longer than all the rest of us.

We Americans have already accumulated so much DDT in our flesh that, according to Department of Agriculture rules, the tissue of our bodies would be labeled not fit for human consumption if it were the flesh of beef or chicken.

We turn our backs on such good advice as the least-read line in any magazine or newspaper today: the one that says, "Warning: The Surgeon General Has Determined That Cigarette Smoking Is Dangerous to Your Health."

I look at my roster of lost friends.

Klein—ran for a train and died of a heart attack.

Swarthout—worried himself into a heart attack.

Blauth—ate a lobster at midnight and had a heart attack.

Schultz—tried to save a pet when his house caught fire. Heart attack.

Grady, Cohen, and Martin simply went to sleep and stayed asleep.

None was old, merely careless. Each was an average American unconsciously *living* himself straight into the cemetery.

Physicians are generally agreed that the principal risks to long life are these:

High blood pressure
High levels of cholesterol and other fatty elements in the blood.

And they are caused by:
Cigarette smoking
Obesity
Under-exercise
Tension and stress
Heredity

Dr. Jeremiah Stamler, Chicago cardiologist, says, "If you are beset by any one of them, your risk of premature heart attack is boosted two to six times above the risk of the person free of such a burden. With a combination of factors, your risk is far higher."

You have two courses of action:

1. You can plunge into a crash program recommended by some friend, publication, or health resort.

2. You can soberly consider each of the factors which put you at risk, and estimate your chance of doing whatever will change them in your favor.

They can all be changed—except one, heredity.

The other factors—high blood pressure, high blood-fat level, obesity, smoking, lack of exercise, etc.—are very vulnerable to persons possessing common sense and uncommon backbones. But how can you escape becoming a vital statistic?

First, what happens when you exercise?

Three things:

1. Your heart beats faster.
2. You breathe faster.
3. You sweat.

These are the physiological reactions which mean that your self-improvement program has started. In short, exercise is a new stress, and your body is adjusting. Call it coping. Every time you exercise (stress your body), your organs try to cope. In a way, it's an educational process, like spring football training. The old team is working together again but it needs smoothing out, needs more experience in togetherness. As in any kind of practice, skill improves and the work becomes easier. This is called training.

What organ most needs training? The heart.

The heart has been described as a four-chambered double pump made of special muscles so powerful that it can beat billions of times with no apparent rest. The top two chambers are depots for the momentary storage of blood. The two bottom chambers are the pumping vessels. Right side of the heart, one pump. Left side of the heart, another pump, but stronger and bigger. They work together, driving jigger-sized jolts of blood into two independent circuits.

*The pulmonary circuit:* This is a simple traffic loop with the heart at one end and the lungs at the other. The right side of the heart pumps dirty blood into the lungs, where it is cleansed, loaded with oxygen, and returned to the heart's left side, ready for another sixty-second journey through your body.

*The systemic circuit:* This is a complicated plumbing network that serves all your systems: organs, bones, skin, the heart itself—you. Its arteries and arterioles carry fresh blood to the thin-walled capillaries—billions of them—that supply your every nerve and muscle fiber. When the feeding phase is over, the same bloodstream picks up waste products and returns to the heart.

The system of arteries and veins that serves the heart muscle itself is oddly absent from most heart-education programs. It is also the *focus* of untold misery.

Its main conduits are the right and left coronary arteries, so named because they make a kind of crown about the heart's top. Within inches, they separate, divide, branch, split, and make cross-connections into an incredible tangle of thousands of blood passages which penetrate every square centimeter of the muscular walls. Like a miniature barrel of worms but with thousands of interconnections, they supply food and oxygen to and remove waste from the heart alone. They survive all kinds of abuse such as coffee, cigarettes, French fries, and stress. One blight they cannot survive is called *atherosclerosis*, a disease in which a kind of gruel accumulates in the lining of these arteries, thickening with the years, hardening, and finally blocking (partially or totally) the passage of blood. We call the result a coronary, an infarct, heart insufficiency, or congestive heart failure.

Life begins with a heartbeat. But what makes the heart beat?

Your heart houses a tiny collection of very special fibers called the S-A *node*. This node uses elements in your blood (such as sodium, potassium, and calcium) to create an electrical charge.

This charge, tiny at first, grows until it no longer can be contained. The node lets go and an excitation wave spreads through both upper heart chambers, and they contract, driving blood into both lower chambers, or *ventricles*.

At the same instant, the impulse is conducted through other special fibers which slow it down a fraction of a second before it races on to encircle the walls of the lower chambers.

These walls now contract like a suddenly clenched fist, squeezing hard, thrusting blood into your arteries.

Already both upper chambers have relaxed and are filling again, and the S-A node is busy in its own mysterious way converting chemicals into another electrical charge.

That is a heartbeat.

The other side of the question is why does a heart *not* beat? There are many reasons, and we can discuss only a few.

1. A heart is served (with food and oxygen) by an extensive network of arteries. The great affliction of this century is the corruption of the inner linings of those arteries by means of an invasion of fat-like cells composed of cholesterol and other fatty substances manufactured by the body. This is the process that may cause the hardening of the arteries called *atherosclerosis,* which acts like scale in a water pipe, reducing the flow as it thickens.

This disease process is serious to the degree that it compromises your blood supply. It can happen simultaneously all over the body or in an isolated organ. Sometimes it affects the leg arteries and the legs turn blue and painful. It may clog the arteries running up the neck to the brain, causing dizziness, loss of memory, and lack of coordination. If the flow in the brain is choked off totally, it is called a stroke. If it happens to a coronary artery, this is called a coronary. Total occlusion is usually fatal. An exception was the astronaut James White, one of the three pilots burned to death in a freak accident at Cape Kennedy in 1967. An autopsy revealed that one of White's coronary arteries had been completely closed. Yet, he had jogged, played hard handball, and lifted weights along with the other astronauts. Space physicians had cleared him as extremely fit. Apparently, collateral circulation within the heart had increased so much that it provided all the blood needed even during severe exertion. White's exercise program is probably one of the reasons.

2. The heart may *not* beat when one of its major arteries is obstructed by a clot. Millions of infinitesimal platelets are in your bloodstream and so are fragments of tissue-stuff called fibrin. Nature put them there for your protection. They are normally healers, piling up around tissue cracks and punctures until the break is mended. Sometimes clots form in a bruised

vessel, then break away and float through the vascular system to lodge in the heart or lungs. Like a stump floating down a river, a clot can get hung up where the stream divides, in shallows, or in a narrowing sluice. Lodgment dams the bloodstream and can affect the legs, the head, the lungs, and the heart. Pain is one result. Paralysis can be another. Death is always a threat. Clots form most readily in persons who do not exercise.

A heart can fail for so many reasons: Valves become corroded and leaky. Capillaries tighten and refuse to transmit food and oxygen to working muscle. Walls over-strain and over-stretch, exhausting their pumping power. Tissue becomes so irritable that the heart's pacemaker goes on a rampage, sending showers of electricity in all directions, making the beat so rapid *(fibrillation)* that no blood is pumped because there is no time between beats for it to fill the chambers. A kidney kicks up. The adrenals discharge too much adrenaline. The ultimate cause of heart failure—and the common denominator that ties all these diseases and accidents together—*is lack of oxygen,* which is to say, *lack of exercise.*

Take a closer look at the risk factors.

## HIGH BLOOD PRESSURE (HYPERTENSION)

High blood pressure is so dangerous that the National Heart Association has mounted an ongoing national campaign to alert the public to its disastrous potential. It causes fatigue, nervousness, palpitation, sleeplessness, dizziness, and headaches. Sometimes the heart enlarges. Nosebleeds and profuse menstrual bleeding are common. Hypertension can ruin a heart or brain; dim the eyes; choke the kidneys; and rupture the linings of blood vessels.

Your cardiovascular system is a closed circuit like your automobile radiator. Blood—like water or coolant—goes round and round, propelled by a pump. If you listen to a heart through a doctor's stethoscope, you can hear it going *lub-dub*. . . . The sound is that of valves slapping shut.

As the heart lub-dubs, blood is forced into the arteries under a pressure that is the result of the heart's volume times its speed of contraction times the speed of its beat. This contraction is called by its Greek name, *systole*. This arterial pressure normally amounts to about 120 millimeters of mercury as measured on a medical instrument called a *sphygmomanometer*.

The period of relaxation in the heart muscle is called a *diastole* (Greek for dilatation). Pressure within your closed system during diastole is produced by the pressure of the elastic walls of your arteries, arterioles, and capillaries. Normally it is about 80 millimeters of mercury.

If your blood pressure, as reported by a physician, is 120 over 80, you probably are without serious vascular disease. The border line between healthy and unhealthy blood pressure is shadowy, but troubles usually become serious (and your doctor gets worried) if your systolic pressure is over 160 and your diastolic is over 95.

Does exercise help? For years, exercise physiologists have maintained that it does, whereas the general run of physicians have been reluctant to agree. The latter's use of drugs often provides substantial benefits. On the other hand, I have read hundreds of reports from members of exercise classes (mostly businessmen) whose personal physicians have said repeatedly that their pressure has been lowered.

Physical directors in YMCAs, who have had wide experience with reconditioning hypertensives (persons with high blood pressure) through exercise, have told me of members of their classes who enrolled with soaring systolic and diastolic rates but became normotensives after a training program.

Scientific research that proves the point has been doubted by many physicians. This is understandable. Their experience is usually limited to the action of drugs. They also seem to have a built-in skepticism about physiological data not offered by another doctor of medicine.

But the logic of physical improvement is irrefutable. Exercise stimulates and massages the arteries, which become more elastic as their muscular walls become more resilient. The flow of blood through them becomes freer and easier. Heating the muscles via exercise enables collateral circulation to develop. Tiny capillaries spread and stretch, feeding increased amounts of blood to nerve and muscle fibers. Because of this greater flow, the "head of steam" generated within the beating heart is reduced. So the blood pressure drops.

Inevitably, the risk of sudden death posed by high blood pressure *is* reduced by exercise.

## HIGH LEVELS OF CHOLESTEROL AND TRIGLYCERIDES

A few years ago the reduction of cholesterol and triglycerides was a moot point. Cholesterol was a fat found in meat and milk products. American arteries were filling with it, according to thousands of postmortem examinations. Theorists said that we should stop eating marbled meat and drinking milk. This looked like a solution until a group of medical men from Louisiana State Medical School in New Orleans went to East Africa and captured a tribe of vegetarian, fruit-eating baboons. Despite the lack of meat and milk in their diet, their arteries were loaded with cholesterol.

Another expedition visited the Masai tribes of Kenya and took blood samples. Masai men are herdsmen who live on whole, fat-rich milk mixed with blood from their cattle. Moving from one grazing ground to another, they walk miles. Their blood showed one of the lowest concentrations of cholesterol on record.

Some years ago, Prof. Vincenzo Lapiccirella, of the University of Florence in Italy, visited tribesmen of Somaliland. They lived exclusively on camel's milk, which is the fattest milk present in nature. He expected to find very high levels of cholesterol in their blood, exceeding the 225–250 level of the average American. To his astonishment, they averaged only ½ the amount of blood cholesterol of the average American. Out of 203 tribesmen examined, not one had heart disease.

So you eat no meat and drink no milk and you may have a high cholesterol count. Or you eat only meat and milk, and your arteries may remain clean. It seemed a mystery.

Recent evidence offers this explanation: Activity makes the difference. Dr. Lawrence Golding, of Kent State University, has authored a long-term study which proves that exercise, if long enough and hard enough, reduces cholesterol and triglyceride levels in humans. Dr. H. J. Montoye, of Michigan State University, has summarized his decade of study of the residents of Lansing, Michigan, by stating that "Blood cholesterol, body fatness . . . and total fat intake all appear to vary together, and are inversely related to physical activity."

Thomas Kirk Cureton, of the University of Illinois, found no improvement when the exercise was casual swimming, softball, badminton, volleyball, bowling, golf, or any leisurely sport. He says the best programs are continuous and rhythmical, such as running, swimming, skating, skiing, cycling, and hiking.

Eliminating animal fats from your diet reduces cholesterol, too, but the Golding study reveals that exercise provides such bonuses as increased strength, a stronger heartbeat, greater vital capacity, a better pulse recovery rate, and lower blood pressure. Therefore the benefit is not an isolated entity but a gratifying complex of physical changes-for-the-better. What is clear is that exercise is vastly more protective than dieting.

## SMOKING CIGARETTES

If you smoke cigarettes, exercise can do nothing for you. What you need is a training program for your willpower. Many friends of mine have said, "I want to quit but I can't. I'm hooked." Then they have a heart attack and it is amazing how quickly they become unhooked. If they survive their first attack—and most do—and adopt sensible, lifetime habits, they can recover and live useful lives.

Switching to a pipe or cigar is an option exercised by many men and a few women. But think twice. The switch reduces coronary risk but increases the peril of oral cancer and peripheral vascular disease. Better quit *cold*.

## OBESITY AND OVERWEIGHT

A previous chapter described the influence of this factor on coronary risk. Weight control has been understood since antiquity. Hippocrates prescribed diet regimes that stressed a moderate food intake and long walks. The body still reacts favorably to his prescription. Hilda Bruch says, "The recommendations are so time-honored and successful, if adhered to persistently, that the only puzzle is why overweight and obesity are still with us."

A word of warning: If you are 30 pounds over your normal weight, don't exercise vigorously. Especially, don't skip rope. Lifting your body off the ground at each skip can impose an intolerable load on your heart. Go on a diet for a couple of months, walk a lot, and *then* skip.

By the way, a woman is supposed to be able to diet and lose weight faster than a man. She usually needs to. In day-to-day dining, she must be careful to eat *less* than her husband.

As a rule, she weighs less, and thus requires less. Hostesses and restaurants routinely serve equal portions. Studies show that, on average, she should consume 900 calories *less* per day than hubby. When couples eat out a lot, the woman invariably ends up overweight. Another fact, usually forgotten, is that our needs decrease as we get older. So therapy can begin when you leave something on your plate.

## STRESS AND TENSION

Stress has been called the big killer, perhaps the most dangerous killer of all.

Stress can be defined as a condition with which the body must cope. Stress can be a request for a raise, a speaking engagement, a confrontation with a fellow employee, a driveway full of snow, a flat tire, a missed airplane flight, a motel reservation that didn't stick, a seat in the balcony when you wanted front row center. Most of us learn to roll with life's punches. We do it so automatically that usually we are not even aware that we are under stress.

A group of men was shown a series of films. As they watched, their blood pressure was recorded. When they watched a film containing suspense scenes, their pressure rose. Watching scenery—it fell. A blonde beauty made love—up. A man lost his job—up. Afterward, not one member of the group admitted that he had felt stress.

Even driving your own car is stress. A research project in Philadelphia wired drivers to portable ECG machines and had them drive through familiar streets. Their heart rates rose to 145 beats per minute. A group of recovered cardiacs were given the same treatment. Their hearts developed premature contractions, irregularities, and fitful acceleration.

Another investigator studied thirty-five truck drivers who had suffered heart attacks, survived, and returned to work.

Five of them suffered repeat infarctions, four of them while on the job. In a recent study of more than 1,000 single-car accidents on California highways, 10 percent were found to be the result of a coronary episode while driving.

"Auto driving represents a significant stress in normal as well as in coronary subjects," says Dr. Samuel Bellet, the investigator and director of the cardiology division of the Philadelphia General Hospital.

Totally unrecognized as stress is the simple fact that one's last name begins with a letter from S to Z. Researchers have learned that people with names that start at the end of the alphabet die sooner than those whose initials are A to R. The reason? More frustration, perhaps. All their lives they have been last in line, last to recite in school, last to get their pay, last in army chow lines. As their resentment builds, they develop stress symptoms.

People under unbearable stress adopt strange coping devices. Some kill their families, their friends, or themselves. Some become catatonic, refusing to move or talk. Dr. Wilhelm Raab, of the University of Vermont, once told me of a thirty-seven-year-old woman who was so upset by the death of her father that she went to bed forever. "She was there for thirty years," he said. "Once, she tried to get up but she was too weak. Her heart rate ranged between a hundred and twenty-eight and a hundred and forty, even in bed. Eventually she died of cancer."

Animals are just as strange.

Take a seagull sitting on a nest of eggs. If an egg is removed, instead of fighting back, she hops out and pulls up grass, adding it to her nest. If two eggs are removed, she doubles the size of her home-improving project. And so on, in direct proportion to the eggs removed.

Take a male stickleback fish. Normally, he digs holes in the bottom, in which his mate can lay her eggs. Each male has his own turf. If he is at home, he attacks any intruder and drives him out. If the intrusion takes place near a boundary between territories, both fish apparently become uncertain of their rights and are violently frustrated. So they dive to the bottom and butt huge holes in it with their heads, forming hundreds of pits.

We have all seen humans butting their heads senselessly against a wall probably for similar reasons.

The overwhelming significance of stress has been acknowledged in the study of heart failure only recently. For many years, the "plumbing" theory sufficed to explain how our pipes choked with sludge, our heart-pump weakened, and how our circulation was blocked by globs of debris floating through our blood vessels.

Apparently there is much more than that to a heart's sudden death.

It now appears that the demise results also from tension and stress. Indeed, one theory holds that stress is the cause of *all* disease.

I was covering the First International Conference on Preventive Cardiology at the University of Vermont for the Associated Press and the *Reader's Digest* when I first met Dr. Hans Selye, the world-famous stress researcher.

He proposed that the scientists present at the conference should look beyond the hydraulic behavior of the bloodstream to the coping action of the body's nerves and the powerful secretions produced by those coping efforts. It was—and still is—a revolutionary thought.

To comprehend his reasoning, a kind of double-barreled thinking now becomes necessary. It's not easy, but let's try.

Your nervous system has two divisions. One division serves the skeletal muscles and is under the control of the brain. It permits you to "will" a movement like scratching your nose or climbing a mountain. The other division performs automatically—it is called the autonomic system—and works willy-nilly in the regulation of "near vision, size of the eye's pupil, constriction and dilatation of blood vessels, rate and force of heartbeat, muscular activities of the digestive tract, emptying the urinary bladder and gallbladder, erection of the penis, occurrence of gooseflesh, and secretion of all glands under nervous control."

This automatic system also has two sub-parts.

*Part 1*—called the *sympathetic* system (it has nothing to do with sympathy)—is a nerve network designed to speed things up, like your heart, your breathing, your bowel movements.

*Part 2*—called the *parasympathetic*—is designed to slow things down, like your heart, your breathing, the rippling of your bowels. If you've heard a doctor talk about the vagus nerve, he's dealing with the automatic computer inside your skin that applies the brakes to a runaway organ.

The human body is thus equipped with an accelerator and a brake. The accelerator provides automatic assistance in emergencies, in moments requiring great bursts of effort and endurance. The brake automatically reduces momentum after a crisis and keeps the organism from spinning its wheels or flying apart. Your problem is to keep both devices operating efficiently. How to do that is still down the road a bit.

Until we get there, consider how your nervous system performs its hurry-or-wait functions.

It acts by producing chemicals which spread into your tissues from the billion (who knows how many) nerve terminals in the organs that are trying to cope. These emergency chemicals are incredibly powerful and intermittently flood their target sites. The hurry-up chemical, called *sympathin*, is almost identical to adrenaline.

The take-it-easy chemical is called *acetylcholine*. Its mission is to spread nerve impulses—but slowly. Always it drags its feet, slowing things down to normal.

Pioneer researchers proved these points years ago when they placed an experimental animal on their operating table. Its normal heart rate was 150 beats per minute. First they cut the sympathetic (hurry-up) nerve (like taking your foot off the accelerator), and the fast heartbeat slowed immediately to 100. Then they cut the parasympathetic nerve (like taking your foot off the brake) and the beat moved back up.

Both systems operate constantly, they decided, balancing each other to maintain the body at its maximum efficiency. Suspend the operation of either (as with a cut nerve or disease) and the other takes over.

Our problem today seems to be that our heart tissues are bathed (some say constantly, some say periodically) by unimaginably potent chemicals, mostly from the sympathetic system, which is trying as never before in history to adjust to the irritants of civilization. Name them and your Fright List will include gadgets that don't work, muggers, telephones, unpaid bills, overcharges, computer errors, ingratitude, divorces, taxes. Together they add up to S T R E S S.

And stress produces an adrenaline-like flood at sympathetic nerve endings all over the body. If the flood is severe, the patient drowns. Dr. Hans Selye has made that very clear.

His realization of this was an accident. Dr. Selye thought he was discovering a new sex hormone, so he injected some promising material into a female rat, expecting sexual changes. Instead, autopsy showed her innards spotted with tiny ulcers, her adrenals swollen thrice their original size, and her lymph system deteriorated.

What could cause such total wreckage? Was it his injection? He tried a different material—formaldehyde—and got the same result. Blindly experimenting, he installed a colony of rats on his icy laboratory roof. One by one, they died from the cold. He put rats in revolving cages and ran them dizzy. He injected them with salt water. The result—always the same. Their insides were messed up, exactly like the previously injected rats. The coincidence inspired a thought that has obsessed Dr. Selye ever since.

The master killer of life, he believes, is stress.

Thus began an amazing story of scientific sleuthing. Selye's first suspect was the pituitary gland. He wondered if its potent overflow might be the mystery killer. In his first test he removed the pituitaries from a batch of rats and stressed the rats with devastating noises, extremes of temperature, and poisons. Their innards remained undisturbed.

In his second test he removed adrenal glands from another group of rats, stressed the animals, and their innards remained remarkably healthy.

He concluded that if stress riddled the organs of intact rats and did not harm the organs of rats whose glands had been removed, then it had to be the pituitary and adrenal reaction to stress that killed his rats.

Dr. Selye named his discovery the Stress Adaptation Syndrome, and said that it works like this:

1. Stress produces an alarm in the body.
2. The pituitary, doing its duty, pours out hormones which signal the adrenals to pour out more.
3. The body adapts to the new situation as best it can, whatever the stress.
4. Finally, under continuing stress, its adaptive power is exhausted. Now the struggling glands swell and rupture. Worn-out organ tissue ulcerates, cells die, and finally the body, too.

All because of too much stress.

Exercise is stress, too. The human body can be overstressed, no matter how perfect a physique or how well-trained an athlete. Coaches call it "staleness."

Dr. Selye says that each of us is endowed with a specific amount of *adaptive* reserve. We use it throughout our lives, and when our adaptive reservoir finally runs dry, we can no longer cope, and we die. That is a gloomy thought, except for one thing: Dr. Selye went ahead with other experiments and learned how the body can be taught to outsmart its glands.

Another disciple of the stress theory was Dr. Wilhelm Raab, who had organized the Burlington Conference. As Professor Emeritus of Experimental Medicine, University of Vermont, and chief of its Cardiovascular Research Unit, he had performed some revealing experiments on both men and animals. Most of these stemmed from his hunch that stress also damaged a man's heart. His reasoning was:

1. Under stressful conditions, the brain activates sympathetic nerve endings within the heart which spew a powerful juice—sympathin—through heart and blood-vessel tissues.
2. Because "civilized" life continually bombards us with stresses, this stepped-up flow continues indefinitely.
3. The molecules which make up this substance from sympathetic nerve endings consume extraordinarily large quantities of oxygen.
4. Their greedy uptake of oxygen added to the normal demands of working heart muscle creates an oxygen shortage.
5. Ages ago the arteries of men were soft and flexible and could expand to accommodate a larger flow of blood (and oxygen), but man's arteries are hardened today and cannot expand. So extra blood is not forthcoming.
6. In the heart, your tissues and the droplets of your "coping" chemicals fight for whatever oxygen is available.
7. The droplets, hungrier, stronger, and constantly reinforced, eventually win.
8. So your starving heart cells wither, ulcerate, and die.

"The plumbing of the heart is of extreme importance, but it is not the whole story," Dr. Raab told me. "The oxygen demand of the heart is dominated completely by the nervous system. On one side, the sympathetic division is wasting oxygen and on the other side the parasympathetic is trying to preserve it. So we have all those hormones being shot, so to speak, in billions of tiny injections, into the heart and blood vessels."

He penciled a diagram of the sympathetic nerves serving the heart, and I saw that they formed a deadly, all-embracing web. "They lock in every single heart muscle cell," he explained. "Their terminals shoot the sympathetic hormone into the heart muscle. Normally, this is very useful, but the discharge increases by one hundred percent under stimulation. When this gets out of hand, it is one of our worst enemies."

I asked him, "Why do some men drop dead suddenly while others survive their first attack?"

"I missed it for fifteen years," he said. "But I learned finally that death happens the day that the arteries cannot expand. They finally reach the point where they are too hardened. The lack of dilatability is the critical element."

Dr. Raab called the corpuscles which make up hormones by the name "wasters." Scientists call them catecholomines. They waste oxygen, the stuff of life. Many authorities think they kill more people than bad plumbing.

Among those who agree are two prominent cardiologists of San Francisco, Drs. Meyer Friedman and Ray H. Rosenman, who have written a book, *Type A Behavior and Your Heart.*

Type A behavior, they say, is what bathes our organs constantly in high-powered hormones. A Type A person is a striver, a deadline-meeter, and a compulsive competitor. Dr. Friedman describes him as having an appetite for numbers, but nobody knows why. "In childhood, he gets a train. Later, he wants more trains. A girl gets a doll and collects more dolls. Numbers become an obsession. The child gets one present and wants another."

When he grows up, he can never say no. He brings papers home from the office, even takes them to bed with him. He is busy, busy, busy. He loves to get Christmas and birthday cards but he is too busy to read them. He skips breakfast. He holds two or three jobs at once. Numbers, numbers, numbers . . . More, more, more . . . It's a good life. Isn't that what America is all about?

Not so, says Dr. Friedman. Smell the flowers. Instead of struggling to tie up all the loose ends, think of how you can stay alive. Dr. Friedman is an authority. Once, he was known as Cannonball Friedman, demanding of himself and others three times as much work as normal. He thinks he saved his life by turning himself into a Type B person, the kind of relaxed and thoughtful being who takes time to be human—and to avoid heart attacks.

A type A person develops high cholesterol levels, high serum fat in the blood, smokes more, has higher blood pressure, and over-drives his endocrine glands. But not easygoing Type B.

Scientists explain it like this:

Emotion rises in the brain's neocortex and limbic system.

Instructions formulated there are switched to the brain's action center for the body, the hypothalamus, or "lower brain." The hypothalamus recognizes this input, analyzes and organizes it, and sends commands to organs, glands, viscera, skin, and muscles, as needed.

Take an example: Maybe you learn of the death of a close friend or relative. Orders go out. The face pales. Tear ducts secrete. Tiny muscles squeeze out moisture. Blood circulation shifts and you may faint.

In anger or fear, signals stream through the entire sympathetic system; glands and nerve endings double their hormonal output. Your tissues are bathed with an overdose of powerful chemicals. You are ready to fight or flee, ready to save your life or give it. This is over-drive.

The trouble with Type A persons, the doctors say, is that they never stop "over-driving." Consequences are assorted disasters. The blood of a Type A person takes about four times as long to be clear of fats after a lobster dinner, for instance, as that of a Type B person. Which means that the lining of his arteries is exposed four times as long to the possibility of penetration by fatty particles, which build oatmealy plaques on the arterial *intima,* or lining.

Once a plaque is formed, fibrin and platelets in the blood (the stuff that makes scabs on your skin) has a tendency to accumulate atop the established plaques, so in effect, your plaques are getting plaques.

Catecholomines from the endocrine glands are in your bloodstream now, and they cause the closing of many capillaries. Wherever this happens permanently, your tissue degenerates. When the capillaries close that have been nourishing those plaques anchored in your arteries, the latter turn to dead tissue. Dead tissue is scar tissue. Scars in your arterial walls are very bad news.

Insulin in excessive amounts may accumulate in your blood. Dr. Rosenman, in *Type A Behavior and Your Heart,* calls insulin the most devastating of all possible problems, leading to the destruction of the artery's lining.

Is there any escape?

Relaxation and exercise!

Dr. Friedman recommends taking no phone calls during an office meeting. If you have three things to do, do only one. Take more time for each event in your day. Try to get the clutter off your desk-top and out of your life. If you're the boss, he says, talk less. "Everybody knows who the boss is. But some men must be talking all the time to show who is boss." If you exercise, don't compete, with others or with yourself. The adrenalin flood that follows a hooked golf shot or a missed strike can kill as fast as shoveling snow.

Are you Type A or Type B? The doctors say you can tell from how you feel about losing.

## LACK OF EXERCISE

Lack of exercise is our last important heart risk factor.

Exercise combats the dangers cited in connection with the plumbing theory, the catecholomine theory, and the Type A theory.

I once served on a discussion panel of distinguished physiologists and physicians. Our subject was "Exercise and Wellness." Challenges came from some doctors in the audience. My position flatly endorsed exercise. They asked, "How can you be so certain?" They inferred that I, a layman, was without credentials and ignorant of what they had learned in medical school.

"I've read the literature, everything written or translated into English," I responded, "and the evidence in behalf of exercise is overwhelming. This is especially true of the last decade. Read it and you must agree."

But they had not read it, not in medical school, not in their practice, for they are healers (not preventers) of disease. With thousands of patients demanding relief from colds, headaches, and infections, they have little time for educational, preventive therapy.

In case your doctor is still ignorant of what the literature is saying, here is the gist of some recent reports.

The most famous study in the field is the one done by Doctors Morris and Raffie on London's bus drivers and conductors. They studied 3,100 men aged thirty-five through sixty-four and concluded that the drivers (who sat all day long) had more heart disease than the conductors (who clambered about the double-deckers). The same doctors also studied 100,000 postal clerks and mailmen. The sedentary clerks had many more attacks than the more active mailmen.

Americans got into research belatedly but soon piled up

impressive statistics. A study of railroad men in the U.S. Northwest revealed that railway clerks had twice as many coronary deaths as section hands. A study of North Dakota farmers and townsmen showed that farmers had half the number of attacks of their less active neighbors. "Persons doing from one to two hours daily of heavy physical activity had only 18 percent of those working not at all or less than one hour," the President's Council summarized.

The U.S. government–backed Framingham Report, for which citizens of Massachusetts have been studied for years, said that "those classified as most sedentary had a coronary incidence rate almost twice that of those who were only moderately active."

In Westchester County in the 1950s, thousands of men were studied in relation to their work. Among them, sudden death came *earlier* to sedentary men than it did to those most active.

In the South, landowners have almost three times as many coronaries as sharecroppers.

In the Midwest, owners who rented their farms to others had 132 coronary attacks per 1,000, whereas fulltime farm hands had only 20 per 1,000.

In an Israeli kibbutz, an important study (because all of its subjects ate the same kind of food at the community table) found that "in all age brackets, in both sexes, sedentary workers had an incidence rate of heart attacks about two to four times as high as did non-sedentary workers."

## WHEN YOUR HEART SKIPS A BEAT

"Skipped beats" are a common complaint of thousands of men and women. "It feels like my heart is turning over," a friend said of his sensations. Laymen call them "skipped beats" because they feel as if the heart is skipping a beat.

Physicians call them *ectopic* beats or *extra systoles.*

Doctors dismiss most skipped beats. Some cardiologists believe a rare kind suggests impending ventricular fibrillation (racing of the heart), which may signal a severe, possibly fatal disturbance. Like many other men who are not as young as they once were, I've felt them after drinking coffee, after exercising, and even after nothing whatever.

And I cured them by increasing my fitness through exercise. Recently a report was presented to a convention of the American Heart Association by two leading American human-performance laboratories. Two teams of eminent researchers were behind it.

They had studied a sample of 196 coronary-prone men. Half had exercised, half had continued their sedentary ways. The exercisers worked out three times a week for eighteen months.

**Results:**

The non-exercisers had as many skipped beats as ever.

The exercisers had significantly *fewer.* Moreover, they could do much harder work than their indolent brothers before experiencing any signs of distress.

My skipped beats disappear when I exercise regularly. When I drink coffee and neglect my workouts, they return. I don't know how dangerous they are, but I do know how to get rid of them.

The President's Council on Physical Fitness and Sports said it clearly in 1972: "Biologically, man is a muscular animal. . . . It is easy to see why man, whose every physical function is affected by movement, may get into serious trouble when he ignores the implications of his biological heritage. Exercise should become a way of life."

Some critics still challenge this good news. They want more research. They mistrust the stories of the benefits of exercise. "You are talking mostly about farmers, railway workers, and athletes," one argued recently. "That kind of work doesn't exist today for ordinary people. Do you mean to say that one hour of exercise a day will protect the heart as well as a ten-hour session with a pitchfork?"

Yes, just as well, and maybe better!

Evidence in the literature is too plentiful to be listed. But the findings are heartening.

In Sweden, a group of hospitalized patients were surveyed for symptoms. Altogether, they named 150 different ailments from which they were suffering. These included palpitations, breathlessness, cold hands, cold feet, dizziness, headaches, deep sighing. Their average was 5.4 symptoms per patient. They were given an exercise program of about one hour a day, several times weekly. At the program's end, their symptoms were counted again: 44 ailments had vanished; 68 had diminished; 21 persisted. The average number of symptoms per patient had dropped from 5.4 to 1.1.

It seems obvious that exercise protects the heart, strengthens it, and offsets the harm caused by catecholomines released in the body's effort to combat stresses. I have experienced how training eliminates irregular and premature beats. I have seen how exercise tames the powerful pituitary and adrenal glands so that their response is not one of panic but one of measured support in time of need.

I think what most convinces me about the effectiveness of exercise is not what men have written in scientific reports but what they have done with their own bodies. And a fine example of such a man is Dr. Hans Selye, who experimented with the Stress Adaptation Syndrome. To develop and prove his theories, he told me, he had tested thousands of rats. When he hazed them with such conventional stress as blowing air blasts in their faces, forcing them to run until exhausted, giving them electrical shocks, and frightening them with the recorded sounds of cat-and-rat battles, his animals sickened and died. Then he took another litter of the same strain and age and gave them a conditioning program. When he was satisfied that their hearts, lungs, and limbs were in peak condition, he harassed them with the same stresses that had killed their brothers. This new batch refused to sicken, refused to die.

Amazed and puzzled, Dr. Selye repeated his experiment like any good scientist. Again his rats took their hazing in stride. Nothing fazed them.

"What happened then?" I asked.

"I decided I'd better get myself in shape fast," he said. "I began to exercise."

When the world's most prestigious authority on stress begins to exercise, I figure he must *know* something. So I exercise, too. But with a difference—with a jump rope.

Exercising with a jump rope is probably the smartest kind of activity there is—particularly for the health of your heart.

"Rope skipping should become a national pastime," says Dr. H. L. Herschensohn, medical columnist for the *Los Angeles Times*. "It has many advantages. . . . It is easy to do, it can be done in privacy whenever convenient, it can be started and stopped at will, and it can be increased gradually without putting undue strain on the heart. When a person skips rope, he can stop the moment he is tired or feels any chest discomfort. He is already home and doesn't have to jog all the way back."

# Epilogue

I shall conclude this book with a confession.

All my life I have had a persistent wish to do everything I attempt better. Nothing I have written, no work performed, whether in business or journalism, has ever really completely satisfied me. I always have wanted to do better.

Some say this is a universal drive for power or pleasure; others have said it represents the soul's search for identification with a higher being. Whatever the cause, I have sought "perfection" in vain.

And so have millions of others. If you too are plagued by a wish to do better, this final message is for you.

Having lived the chair-bound existence of most sedentary men and women, I accidentally discovered the blessing of regular, vigorous exercise, and it changed my life. Then I discovered the jump rope, which made a final and more profound change. Teaching my body to cope with stress has enabled me to measure up more effectively than I had dreamed was possible. It seems that changing one small facet of a busy life permitted improvement in many more areas. Suddenly everything became easier. Frankly, I am not yet where I want to be

(I know I'll never be wholly satisfied) but at least one aspect of my being has been toned to the potential for which it was intended.

In short, I believe that my fitness program has brought my body to its maximum efficiency, freeing my mind and emotions to do their best in other spheres.

My hope is that many persons who read this book will be guided to the same freedom. Scientists have devoted much study to how the mind's climate affects the body. We know that psychosomatic ailments are commonplace. What we understand less well is how the body's climate influences the mind.

Until recently, we had no need to give our bodies a second thought. For millions of years it was a very busy bit of human machinery. Children walked to school, rode stick horses instead of Yamahas, and played sandlot games. Adults traveled by bike or buggy or horseback, hitching and saddling their own steeds in a continuous round of bending and stretching.

Henry Ford and his ilk changed all that, ushering us into a clangorous, push-button world. Today we are house-bound and office-bound. The American eagle no longer flies—he perches. Sitting is our national posture. We move mountains, sitting on a tractor. Our astronauts go to the moon, taking along a glorified golf cart. Sitting, we phone, confer, commute, tour. And all the while, our senses receive a furious bombardment: lights flashing, bells ringing, motors roaring, voices rising, tires screeching, crowds jostling, smells penetrating, headlines booming—until we have nervous systems as potentially dangerous as coiled rattlesnakes in a barrel. For all these sensations impinge upon the brain, which forthwith orders the glandular system to open its floodgates.

Once this Mayday response of adrenaline enabled man to survive by fighting or fleeing. Today, as one attempts to cope, it induces an internal corrosion. No wonder Americans have the highest blood pressure of any people. No wonder heart attacks afflict us like a modern black plague. No wonder that more than one-half of the beds in American hospitals are occupied by *mental* patients.

It has been argued that our forebears had to fight famines, fires, animals, and marauding invaders; that they were no strangers to tension and stress; and that they nevertheless needed no drugs or surgery to help them survive. But they *moved*, from early dawn until evening, like the modern Masai herdsmen of Africa, whose arteries and hearts are among the earth's healthiest.

We too must move, not as our ancestors did, but in accordance with modern needs. This book has already indicated the type and amount of movement that will release you from your bondage to obesity, unwellness, and discontentment with yourself. The principles of the kind of exercise that liberates are worth stressing again:

1. It should be regular.
2. It should be rhythmic.
3. It should be more intense than any work that you do ordinarily. This is called overload.
4. It should be continuous in a mode that alternates periods of work and rest, thus maintaining a heart rate that fluctuates from something less than your maximum to something more than your resting rate.
5. Each exercise session should be introduced by a warm-up and followed by a warm-down.

The immediate result is better health, and this is only the beginning. Exercise enables me to live comfortably with the human unease that obsesses me, and to cope with my secret need to pursue excellence. I once asked Dr. Paul Dudley White to explain the feeling of contentment and freedom that I derived from an active body.

It should be realized by everyone, he said, "that the establishment of positive health and its maintenance by good habits favor a good circulation of blood to the brain, in which are centered not only our memory and our physiological centers, but *our very soul.* Whatever we can do, therefore, to avoid arteriosclerosis in the arteries of our brains, as well as in our hearts . . . will greatly enhance and prolong our usefulness and happiness by keeping our minds and our souls as free as possible from cobwebs, fog, and smoke. We don't need to make a fetish of health habits, but we must recognize that our somatic deficiencies can not only shorten our lives but depress our spirits."

Note that he said there is no need to make a fetish of health habits. In his own life he never did, but he walked and walked, four miles each day. Nor do I, but I skip.

Reread the principles of this liberating exercise—and then, for your own sake, do something. I promise many happy results, including tingling muscles, relaxed nerves, tolerance for the intolerable, and brain cells that sing. And maybe, if Dr. White is right, your very soul will sing too.

# Bibliography

Astrand, Per-Olof. *Health and Fitness*. Stockholm: Swedish Information Service, 1972.

———, and Kaare Rodahl. *Text Book of Work Physiology*. New York: McGraw-Hill, 1970.

Baker, John A. "Comparison of Rope Skipping and Jogging as Methods of Improving Cardiovascular Efficiency of College Men." *Research Quarterly* (American Assoc. for Health, Physical Education, and Recreation, Washington, D.C.), May, 1968.

Blakeslee, Alton, and Jeremiah Stamler. *Your Heart Has Nine Lives*. Englewood Cliffs, N.J.: Prentice-Hall, 1963.

Cascino, Joseph A. *The Effects of a Program of Progressive Rope Skipping on the Cardiovascular Fitness of Adult Men*. Master's Thesis, Temple University, Philadelphia, 1964.

Cooper, Kenneth H. *Aerobics*. New York: M. Evans, 1968.

———. *The New Aerobics*. New York: M. Evans, 1970.

Cooper, Mildred, and Kenneth H. Cooper. *Aerobics for Women*. New York: M. Evans, 1972.

Cureton, Thomas Kirk, Jr. *The Physiological Effects of Exercise Programs on Adults*. Springfield, Ill.: Charles C. Thomas, 1969.

De Vries, Herbert A. *Physiology of Exercise*. Dubuque, Ia.: William C. Brown, 1966.

Johnson, Warren R., and Elsworth Buskirk. *Science and Medicine of Exercise and Sports*. New York, Harper & Row, 1973.

Jones, D. Merritt, Chadwick Squires, and Kaare Rodahl. "Effect of Rope Skipping on Physical Work Capacity." *Research Quarterly* (American Assoc. for Health, Physical Education, and Recreation, Washington, D.C.), May, 1962.

Karpovich, Peter V. *Physiology of Muscular Activity.* Philadelphia: W. B. Saunders, 1959.

Kiphuth, Robert. *How to Be Fit.* New Haven, Conn.: Yale University Press, 1956.

Kraus, Hans, and Wilhelm Raab. *Hypokinetic Disease.* Springfield, Ill.: Charles C. Thomas, 1961.

Lamb, Lawrence E. *Metabolics: Putting Your Food Energy to Work.* New York, Harper & Row, 1974.

———. *Your Heart and How to Live with It.* New York: The Viking Press, 1969.

Mayer, Jean. *Overweight: Causes, Cost, and Control.* Englewood Cliffs, N.J.: Prentice-Hall, 1968.

Myers, Clayton R. *The Official YMCA Physical Fitness Handbook.* New York: Popular Library, 1975.

Morehouse, Laurence E., and Augustus T. Miller, Jr. *Physiology of Exercise.* St. Louis: C. V. Mosby Company, 1959.

Paschal, Jim. *The Effect of a Rope Jumping Program upon Cardiovascular Efficiency.* Unpublished graduate thesis, Los Angeles State College, 1967.

Powell, John T. *The Effects of a Program of Progressive Rope Skipping on Prepubescent Boys.* A graduate thesis supervised by Thomas Kirk Cureton, Jr., at the Summer Fitness Day School of the University of Illinois, 1957.

Prentup, Frank B. *Skipping the Rope for Fun and Fitness.* Boulder, Colo.: Pruett Press, 1963.

*Proceedings of the World Congress for Sports Medicine.* Hanover, Germany, June, 1966.

Raab, Wilhelm, et al. *Prevention of Ischemic Heart Disease.* Springfield, Ill.: Charles C. Thomas, 1966.

Rodahl, Kaare. *Be Fit for Life.* New York: Funk & Wagnalls, 1966.

*Royal Canadian Air Force 5BX Plan for Physical Fitness.* Ottawa: Queen's Printer and Controller of Stationery, 1962.

Skolnik, Peter L. *Jump Rope.* New York: Workman Publishing Co., 1974.

Smith, Paul. *Rope Skipping: Rhythms, Routines, Rhymes.* Freeport, N.Y.: Educational Activities, Inc., 1969.

Steinhaus, Arthur H. *Toward an Understanding of Health and Physical Education.* Dubuque, Ia.: William C. Brown, 1963.

U.S. President's Council on Physical Fitness. *Adult Physical Fitness.* Washington, D.C.: Government Printing Office, 1963.

White, Paul Dudley, and Curtis Mitchell. *Fitness for the Whole Family.* New York: Doubleday & Company, 1964.

Wilt, Fred. *Run, Run, Run.* Los Altos, California: Track and Field News, 1964.

## ABOUT THE AUTHOR

CURTIS MITCHELL was born in Montgomery City, Missouri, in 1902. He attended Westminster College and Columbia University, and during World War II he worked in the War Department's Bureau of Public Relations.

Mr. Mitchell had been vice-president and editorial director at Dell and then at Triangle Publications before the war. In 1945 he became National Director of Advertising, Publicity and Merchandising for Paramount Pictures. Since 1948 he has been a freelance author and editor. In addition to his books *Put Yourself in Shape, The Joy of Jogging,* and *Fitness for the Whole Family,* Curtis Mitchell has published hundreds of articles on a variety of subjects in *Reader's Digest* and other leading magazines.

The author and his wife, Zelpha Piper Mitchell, have two daughters and live in Florida.